Are you being duped?

# Are you being
# DUPED?

## Kent Philpott

Earthen Vessel
Publishing

EVANGELICAL PRESS

 EVANGELICAL PRESS

 Earthen Vessel
Publishing

**Evangelical Press**
Faverdale North, Darlington, DL3 0PH  England
**Evangelical Press USA**
PO Box 825, Webster NY 14580  USA
email: sales@evangelical-press.org
**www.evangelicalpress.org**

**Earthen Vessel Publishing**
289 Miller Avenue,
Mill Valley, CA  94941  USA
**www.earthenvessel.net**

Co-published by Evangelical Press and Earthen Vessel Publishing
First published 2004

*British Library Cataloguing in Publication Data available*
**ISBN 0 85234 557 7**

To my twin daughters
Laura Elizabeth and Jenna Maree
who turn fourteen years of age
on the day of this dedication, and to
their mother, my wife, Lisa Maree

Other titles by the author

*Are you really born again? A study of true and false conversion*
*Why I am a Christian*
*For pastors of small churches*

# Contents

# Preface

I have been duped. I have been deceived, lied to, tricked, conned and swindled. The question is: Have you been duped, too?

The duping I am speaking of goes to the core of our existence — it is by no means trivial. This helps explain why I might be so bold as to use the word 'duped'.

I take my cue from Jesus. He directly confronted people and, without compromise, told them they had been duped. For instance, Jesus frequently used the phrase, 'Woe to you', and 'woe' was a serious word back then. The 'woe' statements did not come from anger on Jesus' part, though he did get angry on several occasions. Instead, Jesus attempted to break down walls because eternal life or death was at stake.

In several chapters, I include stories in which Jesus directly and personally opposed error. I am hoping to do a little of the same. A few people helped me to see that I was blind, deaf, lost and rebellious. They helped me to see that I had been duped, and they were not often polite about it. Of course, I have nothing against politeness, but I was not the kind of man who would be moved by sentiment and sweet moralizations.

Jesus did not exactly break new ground. The Old Testament prophets had also been confrontational. Consider this statement from the prophet Jeremiah: 'The heart is deceitful above all things, and desperately corrupt; who can understand it?' (Jer. 17:9). He said 'the heart' — which for a Jew meant the centre or core of their being — is deceitful and desperately corrupt. How strong can you get? Knowing that few, if any, would welcome his message, Jeremiah then asked, 'Who can understand it?' We also do not realize how our hearts can be deceived. In this book I hope to explain something of how and why this deceit works. To summarize, we are deceived and delusional because we are blind, dead, duped and headed down the wrong road. As the man of wisdom said, 'There is a way which seems right to a man, but its end is the way to death' (Prov. 14:12).

In my younger years, I probably would not have been able to write a book like this. (This book began with a series of sermons I preached in the summer of 2001 at Miller Avenue Baptist Church in Mill Valley, California.) I would not have had the courage to be so forthright, worrying too much about people's reactions. Now, somewhat saltier in my sixty-first year, I worry less about being rejected by people and more about doing my job as a gospel preacher. Throughout most of my ministry, I wanted everyone to appreciate me, so I preached like the grandfatherly/therapist/fuzzy-warm comforter many people want in a minister — telling everyone they were okay, I was okay and everything would be all right.

This book has nothing to do with 'good' and 'bad' people. Its thrust has to do with being tricked and, good or bad, we are all vulnerable. The best, the wisest and the purest of us can be deceived and duped.

Perhaps some of you think I am being arrogant. Christians are sometimes accused of being arrogant, with their declarations that Jesus Christ, and only Jesus Christ, is 'the way, and the truth, and the life' (John 14:6). However arrogance is the making of unwarranted claims with a superior kind of attitude. Jesus did not do so. He merely spoke what is true and those who love and follow him hope to do the same, with love and humility.

As I said, I do not come to this as one who has not been duped — and I did the biggest con job on myself. I do not blame my parents, the government, the schools, the devil, or anyone or anything else. The fact is that I wanted to justify my self-centred ways and rebellion. I wanted to live a 'free' life without restraint, think my own thoughts, and all the rest. But there was someone out there who saw the dumb, hopeless little sheep I was and sought after me, found me and has been opening my eyes ever since to the incredible extent to which I had been duped.

As I look back, I realize I did not know what I was doing. I did not see that I was acting against my own best interests. I did not see that I was engaged in a struggle against my Creator. This is the way it is with all of us — we are engaged in a process of spiritual suicide. This one thing we all have in common as human beings — we can oppose ourselves and reject the witness of God. It may be said that this is what the 'unforgivable sin' is all about (see Luke 12:8–12). Therefore, I hope the tenor of this book reflects the gracious words of Jesus who, while nailed to the cross, said, 'Father, forgive them; for they know not what they do' (Luke 23:34).

This book is a ministry project of Miller Avenue Baptist Church. Maggie Bates transcribed the taped sermons and did a marvellous job. Katie Coddaire and Christina Rose worked through each chapter twice, editing and rewriting. I owe these three wonderful Christian ladies a great deal.

David Clark of Evangelical Press took considerable interest in this book and offered a number of helpful suggestions, including the title. Pete Cooper of EP developed the cover and his work is much appreciated.

Janice Van Eck of Ontario, Canada, made the final edit and prepared the manuscript for printing — and how I appreciate her work! Thank you, Janice.

Throughout the book, I refer to San Quentin Prison. For the past twenty-one years, I have been a volunteer in various chapel programmes and for the last seven years I have coached the prison's baseball team.

The Bible version used is the Revised Standard Version (RSV). Over the years I have used many different translations, chiefly the New International Version (NIV), but in recent years I have been preaching with the RSV. Now I have begun using the English Standard Version (ESV) but I appreciate the RSV's classical style and excellence in translating the Greek manuscripts. I have discovered that no translation is perfect; the RSV has its problems, yet overall I find it a useful translation.

I welcome your comments and feedback. Feel free to contact me through the Miller Avenue Baptist Church website at www.w3church.org or by email at kentphilpott@comcast.net

*Kent Philpott*
*December 2003*
*Mill Valley, California*

# CHAPTER 1

# You have been duped if you think you are the 'master of your fate and the captain of your soul'

A n article in the *San Francisco Chronicle* (12 June 2001) about the Oklahoma City bomber, Timothy McVeigh, was the catalyst for the series of sermons upon which this book is based. McVeigh quoted William Ernest Henley's poem 'Invictus'. He singled out the last two lines of that famous poem, 'I am the master of my fate: I am the captain of my soul.'

A cherished possession of mine is a book of poetry my grandmother gave me on 2 August 1984. As a teenager I treasured this book and it was here that I first encountered 'Invictus':

> Out of the night that covers me,
> Black as the Pit from pole to pole,
> I thank whatever gods may be
> For my unconquerable soul.
>
> In the fell clutch of circumstance
> I have not winced nor cried aloud.
> Under the bludgeonings of chance
> My head is bloody, but unbowed.
>
> Beyond this place of wrath and tears
> Looms but the Horror of the shade,

And yet the menace of the years
Finds, and shall find, me unafraid.

It matters not how strait the gate,
How charged with punishments the scroll.
I am the master of my fate:
I am the captain of my soul.

Those last two lines were Henley's main point — he imagined that he was in charge and in control of his life.

Henley was apparently convinced that there was nothing in all the creation that determined anything for him, even if circumstances were beyond his control. In the face of whatever might come, it was still he and he alone who mastered how he would respond to the world around him. That is perhaps the best light that could be put on it, but it is fanciful at best, and unrealistic. It is a false bravado — a whistling in the dark. Ultimately neither Henley, McVeigh, nor anyone else, is in control of anything that has to do with fate and soul. And by this, I do not deny free will, which we have plenty of. But it is limited and securely bounded on all sides. We have only enough free will to get ourselves into trouble, not enough to save us.

## What 'Invictus' meant to me

I read 'Invictus' three or four dozen times in my life. I thrilled to the idea of it and memorized those last two lines, just like McVeigh might have. I brought them to mind at key moments and I exulted when I thought of the words. Yes, the human spirit, how incomparable we are, 'bloody, but unbowed.' In my mind would be some event that happened at school, a challenge to a fight from some gang member, the fear I had of failing at sports or the dread of being in a new school with no friends. Then I would remember those words and take comfort from them.

The poem's last two lines are what Timothy McVeigh quoted in the press release that he gave out and then read just moments before his execution. But he was strapped to a stretcher in the execution chamber. He was powerless while leather straps held him firmly on his back. Then lethal venom was injected into his vein. He turned out not to be the captain of his soul or the master of his fate. In reality, he was the victim of his ignorance. He was the victim of his fears. He was the victim of his lusts. He was the victim of his anger. The ignorance, fears, lusts and anger were his own; he is responsible before God and man.

## The escorted convict

Once in a while I refer to Clint Eastwood as the 'great prophet'. Do you remember one of Eastwood's famous lines in the first *Dirty Harry* movie: 'A man must know his limitations'? Now, I am not putting Eastwood in the class of the biblical prophets, and maybe I ought to delete the adjective 'great', but there is truth in the statement. Most of us do not know our limitations until we are like one convict I saw being escorted across the lower yard of San Quentin Prison.

It was before a baseball practice. I was at the prison earlier than usual hoping to get the equipment cage out and the gear set up. I was with one of the guys on our team, a seasoned convict. He is white, shaved bald, with tattoos seemingly covering his body — some of them X-rated. We were trying to get a guard to open the equipment room when we heard the shout, 'Escort!' A convict was being escorted right by where we were standing. What this means is that anyone within earshot is to go to the nearest wall. I always go to the wall, turn around and watch. My convict companion went to the wall but faced it. He said, 'The reason I face the wall is that I don't want anybody to think I have a plan in my mind that I might carry out while a man is coming by.'

The escorted man had a chain around his mid-section. This was attached to a chain that bound his wrists, while another chain secured his ankles and left him just enough slack to shuffle along. The officers on each side of him wore clear plastic facemasks, metal helmets and flack jackets, while an officer right behind him held a canister of pepper spray just inches from the back of his head.

I asked my companion what was going on. He said, 'This man just got here and he is going up to the adjustment centre before being put on condemned row. Every convict who goes to the row is housed in the A.C. for two to four years so they learn how to live knowing they are going to die. It is not an easy adjustment. I know because I have had to listen to the screaming that comes out of there for fifteen years.'

I noticed that the escorted convict was glancing all around, and I commented on it. My player explained, 'This is the last clear view of blue sky he'll likely ever see, and he knows it.'

The convict was a white man about twenty-five or twenty-six years of age. He had what I would call a computer-science, rocket-science look to him — an intelligent-looking man. He was rather short and stocky, with glasses, black hair and a clean-shaven face. He was dressed in an orange jumpsuit. It seemed to me he was looking furtively at the grass of the ball field — the last grass he might ever see. His eyes roved up and down, side to side. There were seagulls flying overhead and he intently followed their flight. He was desperately looking everywhere. You could just see that he was trying to capture as many glimpses as he could of the outside world before entering the adjustment centre. He was certainly not the master of his fate; he was not the captain of his soul. But neither am I.

In the twenty-first chapter of John is the record of a very unusual statement. It reminds me of that condemned man at San Quentin, McVeigh, myself, and, if you can be honest about it, it will remind you of yourself too. Jesus said to Peter, 'Truly, truly, I say to you, when you were young, you girded yourself and walked where you would; but when you are old, you will stretch out your hands, and another will gird you and carry you where you do not wish to go' (John 21:18). Jesus was basically telling Peter how he would die and that when that moment came Peter would be powerless to do anything about it.

Do we need other illustrations of the fact that we are not the master of our fate, nor the captain of our soul? We do, because there are powerful forces tempting us to think otherwise.

## Jeremiah's analysis of the human condition

Consider Jeremiah 17:19. The prophet wrote, 'The heart is deceitful above all things, and desperately corrupt.' The King James Version has 'wicked' instead of 'corrupt', but modern translations have the better rendering, 'corrupt'. Jeremiah meant that we are deceived and corrupt from within. It is not external but internal. This is evident to most of us, especially those who, by God's grace, have seen through their delusions. This powerful, mysterious and baffling spiritual and emotional condition is why we are so vulnerable to being duped. Can you prove otherwise?

Jeremiah understood how harsh his analysis would sound to his own listeners so he added, 'Who can understand it?' In other words, 'Who will believe what I say? Who is ever going to acknowledge that this is true?'

'Corrupt' is not a word we readily apply to ourselves. Its meaning implies that there is something rotten at our core, something about us that is wicked and depraved. Certainly humans are capable of truly loving acts, thoughts and feelings — this I understand and appreciate. But there is another dimension to us, a dark side, and to ignore it is a mistake.

Do you read a daily newspaper or watch television news broadcasts? It does not take long to realize that there is something wrong in our society. Maybe it is time to give up on the theory that we are, in terms of evolutionary processes, continually improving. We may want to adjust that theory since it is obviously not the case. But who can understand it?

And, more than that, who can admit it personally? How does it come across when I say that *you* are corrupt, that *you* have been deceived, that *you* have been duped? It is better to know it now than discover it later, because one day, you will know it.

This is not to say you are a 'bad person'. But denying what is true does not enhance how we feel about ourselves. I know that those who struggle with issues of security or self-esteem will perhaps wince at this, yet it is the truth and we must face it.

## Isaiah's analysis of the human condition

Now consider Isaiah, another of the Hebrew prophets. If I have not convinced you from the prophet Jeremiah, if I have not convinced you from knowledge of yourself, if you are still unconvinced though you look around at a chaotic and desperate world, if you still fail to see the corruption and the deception that is in the human race, perhaps the prophet Isaiah will convince you.

> A voice says, 'Cry!'
>     And I said, 'What shall I cry?'
> All flesh is grass,
>     and all its beauty is like the flower of the field.
> The grass withers, the flower fades,
>     when the breath of the Lord blows upon it;
>     surely the people is grass.
> The grass withers, the flower fades;
>     but the word of our God will stand for ever (Isa. 40:6–8).

In typical biblical fashion, first there is the bad news, then the good. God reminded Isaiah that the grass withers and the flower fades, and so do we. How many birthdays do you have left? Perhaps you do not have any.

Compare photos of yourself: one taken ten years ago with a recent snapshot. What do you see? You are withering and fading. Try as you might, you cannot do anything about it. And one day you will stand before the one who made you and to him you must give an account. Yes, you will do this, and you are deceived if you think you will not. Though the grass withers and the flower fades, 'the word of our God will stand for ever'.

## 'But wait'

Someone will protest, 'Wait a minute. We can freeze the body now.' Cryonics is the term used for this process. You can have your body frozen and then later on, when medical science has advanced further, a technician will thaw you out and administer the appropriate miraculous cure. Or, tissue will be taken from your frozen body and you will be cloned. Do we really think that all we are is in our DNA? Maybe duped people do.

I am not sure we can count on cryonics. I am not sure there will be sufficient energy, space or goodwill to accommodate everyone. I am not sure there will be technicians around caring enough to handle it all. A flimsy hope indeed!

What about stem-cell research? Medical science is advancing very rapidly after all. And what about the news of cancer cures? We have good news coming and we also have advanced knowledge on how to care for ourselves through nutrition, exercise, and so on. I am not confident that there is going to be a cure for all the deadly diseases. I am not sure that you can count on medical science to make it possible for you to live for ever. Failing all this, some suggest that aliens will arrive with knowledge that will put us beyond the grip of death. I doubt that is going to happen either. Do the words of Jeremiah apply to you? 'The heart is deceitful above all things.'

Maybe you have not fallen for the fanciful solutions to death currently being paraded around the popular landscape like those mentioned above. But perhaps your heart is deceiving you with the hope that you are the master of your fate and the captain of your soul. If you still think so, maybe this last point will be of some value to you.

## A third analysis of the human condition

Examine Hebrews 9:27. The writer of Hebrews, under the inspiration of the Holy Spirit, wrote that 'it is appointed for men to die once, and after that comes judgement'. The author means there are no second chances, no coming around again and no putting off death and judgement. How we dread the thought of death!

A woman in her mid-sixties, whose husband had died several years earlier, visited me on the advice of her daughter. She was struggling to get over her loss. One of the reasons she was in distress was that she had been gripped by the fear of her own dying. During the course of our conversation I said to her, 'This fear is a very real one.' I did not say, 'Oh, its okay. You're young. You're healthy. You haven't even reached the average age of mortality for women in America. You are about ten years from that.' I was not going to give her some cheap comfort to make her feel all right for an hour or two. I wanted her to understand that her fear was a very real one.

She became uncomfortable. Beads of sweat gathered on her forehead. She had difficulty — emotional difficulty — handling the reality that she would die and she could not do anything about it. We are duped if we think we are somehow going to avoid our own death. In our youth and our strength, we feel we will never die. But we will.

The Creator appointed us to die 'once' — once, and there is no coming back. Some say, 'Well, there is reincarnation. I will come back.' You have been duped if you think that you will. Reincarnation is a false hope. You will die and you will not come back. Here is what will happen after you die: 'and after that comes judgement.'

Judgement! You will stand before the judgement seat of God, naked and alone, with nothing in your hands but your own sin and guilt. If this bothers you then you are not far from the kingdom of God. The worst thing that could happen is that this truth should have no impact on you at all. You are in great danger if you can easily shrug it off. Judgement is the bad news. However, the passage is not yet complete.

The twenty-eighth verse gives us the good news: '... so Christ, having been offered once to bear the sins of many, will appear a second time, not to deal with sin but to save those who are eagerly waiting for him' (Heb. 9:28). The corruptness that leads us into all manner of strange behaviour and into the confused, twisted thinking that moves us to rebellion and lawbreaking, Jesus took upon himself at the cross. 'Bear the sins of many' means that he took our death, that eternal death, upon himself. He took the punishment, the condemnation, even the hell we would have to endure, upon himself so that we would not have to. Why? Not for anything we ever did or ever will do, but because he loves us. This is the greatest and most wonderful truth.

## Hopelessness or hope?

The Scripture does not show us the hopelessness of the fact that we will die and then face judgement without revealing the hope that is provided in the gospel. Short of the gospel, there is no hope. Here is the true and solid hope of the gospel — Jesus Christ has been 'offered once to bear the sins of many'. All our sins have been placed upon Jesus, every one. Every sin, mystically, spiritually and actually, placed upon Jesus and for ever buried with him — that means gone. And he also rose from the dead. He is the living Saviour who will return and take those who have been spiritually born again to be with him.

Hebrews says that Jesus will appear a second time. He is not coming to deal with sin a second time, but 'to save those who are eagerly waiting for him'. I love those words — 'who are eagerly waiting for him'.

One of the ways you can spot a Christian is that he or she is eagerly waiting for the return of Jesus. There is no fear of it. Many people are rattled, even angered, by the idea of the return of Jesus. It just makes them mad. Do you know why? They are afraid of judgement. That was also true of me at one time. I would hear talk of the return of Jesus and it did not thrill me at all. I tried to laugh it off as pious talk and 'churchy' language. I would then lie to myself and think that if it actually happened I would be okay.

If you are not looking forward to the return of Jesus, a most horrible dread will fill you when he does return — or you will die before that great event. Either way, you will know then that you have been deceived. You will know, entirely too late and beyond any question, that you are neither the master of your fate nor the captain of your soul.

## What do we control?

There is one other major area we do not have control over and that is conversion itself. By the word 'conversion' I am referring to becoming a Christian. Conversion is popularly known by the term 'being born again'. Here is perhaps the biggest issue of all. We cannot convert ourselves — God himself brings about conversion.

One of the central doctrines of the Bible is the sovereignty and grace of God. By this is meant that God freely initiates and completes conversion. It is his work alone and is not based on anything that we do to accomplish it. I do not mean that God controls each and every act, word and thought. But he must call us, choose us and elect us. We cannot simply decide that we will become Christians. This runs counter to what most people think. Many imagine that 'If I am baptized then I will become a Christian and go to heaven when I die.' Or they think that 'If I join the church, or if I do good deeds, or if I stop sinning, or if I pray the "sinner's prayer", then this will do it.' It will not, and you are duped if you think so.

Consider the term 'born again'. This metaphor indicates that conversion is not something we achieve on our own. We had nothing to do with our physical birth and the same is true for our spiritual birth. It is the work of God. First, the Holy Spirit must show us that we have sinned against God and give us the desire to turn away from our sin. Jesus said that the Holy Spirit would convict us of sin (John 16:8). Then God gives us the faith to trust in Jesus (Rom. 10:17; Eph. 2:8–9). And no one can come to Jesus unless the Father draws him or her (John 6:37,44,65). It is a mistake to think that conversion — the new birth — is within our control. Some Christians who are unclear on this point will often say (just as I did for twenty-nine years of ministry), 'It is your decision. You choose. The responsibility is yours.' This implies that we can control salvation, the forgiveness of sins and conversion itself. We do not control it and the deception on this point usually results in a spurious or false conversion. Many people have been deluded into thinking that something they do (baptism or praying some prayer) is enough to convert them. God alone brings spiritual life. God converts. This is why we present the good news of Jesus: that the Holy Spirit may bring people to Jesus. As Paul wrote to the Roman church, 'So faith comes from what is heard, and what is heard comes by the preaching of Christ' (Rom. 10:17).

It is of supreme importance that you reject the concept that you are in control of your fate.

# CHAPTER 2

# You have been duped if you think the grave is the end

I t is uncomfortable to be challenged regarding what we believe. Beliefs, ideals and philosophies of life go directly to the centre of our being — especially if the subject is religious or political in nature. Why are we like this? Perhaps it is a lack of self-esteem, ego strength or maturity. Then again, fear may play a role as well. Personally, I can be very sensitive if I am questioned too closely about what I hold to be true.

## An appeal

When I was younger, I was not very resilient. I was less sure of myself and my beliefs were practically untouchable. As we mature, however, we discover it is okay not to be right about everything. Hopefully we also have enough grace to be able to change if necessary.

Why do we cling to what is wrong anyway? When we cling to error, it eventually harms us. This cannot be truer than when it comes to death, and by death, I refer to both physical death and spiritual death. To come at it another way, let me ask, 'How willing are you to embrace truth? Will you do so though it might embarrass you for various stands you have taken in the past?' I hope you will have a greater interest in truth than in protecting cherished, though false or inadequate beliefs.

Or, please consider this question: How sure are you, if you believe that the grave is the end, that you are right? Oh, you may believe it with all your heart and soul — but how do you *know* you are right? Do you have any proof of your position? Are you willing to risk absolutely everything?

## Atheists

Atheists are growing in number and are even forming clubs — institution-alizing, if you will. They are not afraid to make their position known. Many atheists are completely persuaded by evolutionary thought and feel they could therefore never become Christians. They do not understand that many Christians, and I mean Bible-believing Christians, accept much of what goes under the name of evolutionary theory. There are genuine disagreements among Christians about evolutionary theory, but many Christians hold to what good science says about the age of the universe and this planet. Most Christians, however, do not believe one species can evolve into another (macro-evolution) but they do accept that life forms change (micro-evolution), which is the core of evolutionary thought. The sciences should not determine what we think about God's existence; rather, the sciences should serve to inform us of the majesty of God.

And then religious people, ancient and contemporary, have embarrassed themselves so much that I can see why people avoid anything to do with God, church and religion. God has received a lot of bad press over the years, and so have those who say they believe in him. (Somehow, people think that Christians are perfect and if they are not, well, there goes the whole thing.) On the other side of it, atheists have something less than a clean record. A little humbleness goes a long way towards arriving at the truth. But I especially appeal to the atheist, since atheists would logically believe the grave is the end — please take a fresh look at the claims of Christ. You cannot be absolutely sure of your atheism, of course, but I understand and appreciate your position.

## Is there proof of life after death?

While reading the *Evangelical Times* (published in England by a sister organization of Evangelical Press), I came across an article about a scientific study that seemed to show that there was an afterlife. But the reviewer, a Christian, was not convinced.

The study had been conducted with people who had 'died' on an operating table and who later reported various experiences they had 'while they were dead'. Some saw a white light, some a saintly figure and others a frightening figure. A few reported that they felt they were slipping into hell, or that they saw loved ones, and so on. The authors of the study concluded: 'This proves there is an afterlife.'

But the reviewer of the study, with whom I agree, reasoned: 'If you really died, you would not come back.' Dead is *dead*. We do not know the complex chemical, electrical and biological processes that go on in the mind and body as a person begins to die. A safe and sane theory is: 'If you really had died you would not come back.' I do not want to be guilty of holding to quasi-scientific evidence that there is life beyond the grave. I would rather appeal to the Scriptures.

## Jesus and resurrection

The Sadducees were a religious/political party that had considerable power in first-century Judaism. The leading priests (those who had control of the temple worship) were mostly Sadducees and they did not believe in life after death. For them, the grave was the end. They knew, however, that Jesus believed in the resurrection of the dead and they approached him one day with a bizarre question designed to cast disparagement on his teaching. The Sadducees asked this question:

Teacher, Moses wrote for us that if a man's brother dies and leaves a wife, but leaves no child, the man must take the wife, and raise up children for his brother. There were seven brothers; the first took a wife, and when he died left no children; and the second took her, and died, leaving no children; and the third likewise; and the seven left no children. Last of all, the woman also died. In the resurrection whose wife will she be? For the seven had her as wife (Mark 12:19–23).

The ridiculousness of the situation, they may have calculated, must convince Jesus that resurrection was an impossible notion. Maybe they hoped Jesus would sputter and fume, or perhaps even side with them. Maybe they hoped to prevent Jesus from siding with the Pharisees, another political/religious group — and the Sadducees' main opposition — who did believe in resurrection. We do not precisely know what their objective was, but Jesus gave the Sadducees a sharp response:

Is not this why you are wrong, that you know neither the scriptures nor the power of God? For when they rise from the dead, they neither marry nor are given in marriage, but are like angels in heaven. And as for the dead being raised, have you not read in the book of

Moses, in the passage about the bush, how God said to him, 'I am
the God of Abraham, and the God of Isaac, and the God of Jacob'?
He is not God of the dead, but of the living; you are quite wrong
(Mark 12:24–27).

The response Jesus gave to the Sadducees applies equally to others
who believe the grave is the end. The Sadducees had revealed that they
did not know the Scriptures for they clearly teach the resurrection. They
also did not know the power of God. When God spoke to Moses out of
the burning bush (Exod. 3:1–6), Abraham, Isaac and Jacob had all lived
and died at least five centuries before. Yet, God was declared their God,
present tense. In that one passage from the Law, the part of the Hebrew
Bible the Sadducees *did* accept as inspired, it is shown that the three
great patriarchs of Israel were living — God had to have raised them from
the dead! Indeed, the Sadducees, and those who believe like them, were
quite wrong.

Could the God who, in an instant, created the universe from nothing
then not have power over death, which is merely a sub-system in the
scheme of life? No, the Creator of life and death is sovereign over both. It
follows that the fundamental reason for believing the grave is the end is
rooted in a basic misunderstanding of who God is.

## Paul and the resurrection

Paul, a first-century Jew, a reluctant convert to Christ and the author of
many New Testament books, wrote to the church at Corinth: 'If in this life
we who are in Christ have only hope, we are of all men most to be pitied'
(1 Cor. 15:19). At this point, the resurrection of Jesus had occurred and
Jesus had appeared many times to the disciples and even to at least one
non-believer, his half-brother James. Jesus had appeared to Paul himself,
a persecutor of those who believed Jesus was the Messiah, while he was
on his way to trouble Christians in Damascus. Paul encountered the living
Christ first-hand — he knew therefore that Jesus was alive.

The reality of the resurrection of Jesus had enormous consequences for
Paul. It meant abandoning much of what he had grown up with as a Jew.
Christ's resurrection could lead to no other conclusion but that Jesus was,
indeed, the Messiah of Israel. Paul knew that a denial of the resurrection
of Jesus would be a lie so he continues: 'But in fact Christ has been raised
from the dead, the first-fruits of those who have fallen asleep' (1 Cor. 15:20).

Paul is asserting that Jesus was the first to rise from the dead ('fallen asleep' is a euphemism for 'died').

Did you know that Jesus rose from the dead on the day of the Jewish Feast of First-Fruits? There are seven major Jewish feasts celebrated each year and the Feast of First-Fruits has to do with the first harvest (the barley harvest). Jesus was the 'first' to be raised from the dead. It is an interesting point especially when you realize that he was crucified on Passover (the day when the Passover lamb was sacrificed to commemorate the Exodus from Egypt under the leadership of Moses) and buried on the Feast of Unleavened Bread (when sin was symbolically removed from each Jewish house). You begin to think that this was not all coincidental.

Jesus rose 'first' from the dead. Our own resurrection will be the fruit that comes after, or the second fruit. Our assurance of life beyond the grave depends upon the resurrection of Jesus.

## Is there proof for the resurrection?

But what proof is there for the resurrection of Jesus? Ultimately the proof comes to us through the witness of the Holy Spirit. By this I mean that the Holy Spirit of God must show us. We will never find it out any other way. Many people know that what *appears* to be concrete is not as reliable as that convincing work of the Holy Spirit. We might question what we see, feel, touch, smell or hear but we will not deny the resurrection of Jesus once we know him as our Saviour and Lord.

Yet, there are substantial proofs of the resurrection; many are quite compelling. For instance, there is the issue of what happened to the physical body of Jesus. The sepulchre where his body was laid had been sealed in the traditional Jewish way with a large rock and mortar, and posted with Roman guards. On the following Sunday morning, the tomb was found to be empty. No one ever did find a body, though it would have been in the interest of the enemies of Jesus to produce one. The religious authorities would not have taken the body — that would have given ground to the claims Jesus had made that he would rise from the dead. If, despite the Roman guard at the tomb, the disciples had stolen the body, would such a fraud have issued in the events that later took place in the lives of those men? So, what did happen to the body of Jesus? This is one proof.

Then, the first witnesses to the resurrection were women. In the culture of that day, women had no legal standing as witnesses and beyond that had generally very low status. Yet, all of the Gospel writers report that women were the first at the grave and the first to witness the resurrected Christ. Why report this unless it was absolute fact and incontrovertible?

Additionally, there is the dramatic change in the downhearted, fearful disciples. The death of Jesus was a terrible blow to them — executed as a criminal by the hated Romans. At the time of his arrest and the subsequent trials, the apostles scattered and hid, fearful they might receive the same harsh treatment as their Master. But Jesus appeared to them alive and in the flesh, and they were never the same afterwards. When you read the accounts of this in the Gospels, you do not get the impression that the disciples conned themselves into believing this. They were not so heartbroken that they needed to resurrect Jesus 'in their hearts', as some have supposed.

Religious literature often sounds syrupy and other-worldly. The encounters between the resurrected Christ and the disciples that we find in the four Gospels lack the fanciful, mystical kind of language that would be used if they were trying to 'sell' a story they had concocted. The reporting is essentially unadorned and matter-of-fact narrative. It has occurred to me that if I had been able to edit the New Testament, I would have insisted on giving more punch to the accounts of the resurrection.

It comes as a surprise to some, but Jesus had a half-brother named James. He was a child of Joseph and Mary and probably was the next oldest to Jesus. This birth order is indicated by James' being named first in the lists of Jesus' four male and at least two female siblings (Matt. 13:55–56; Mark 6:3). This half-brother James, though not a believer during the earthly ministry of Jesus, not only became a believer afterwards but also became the first pastor of the Jerusalem church. This is significant because during his earthly ministry Jesus' family thought he had mental or emotional problems (Mark 3:21). No family members, except his mother Mary, are ever mentioned as being disciples in the Gospel accounts. But, all of a sudden, James is part of the church and numbered with the disciples. How did this happen? Well, remember, one of the resurrection appearances was to James (1 Cor. 15:7).

There are many other evidences of the resurrection of Jesus, but no one can be argued into the kingdom of God. Reason and logic, though not antithetical to faith, cannot produce it. Miracles are not necessary to faith, either. But the person who has tightly closed his or her mind to the possibility that Jesus is the living Lord is in trouble.

## Why we gamble

Why would someone gamble all of eternity that the grave is the end? I use the word 'gamble' deliberately because it is exactly that, a gamble. The Bible offers a number of answers for such a reckless attitude.

First, look at the beginning of Psalm 14:1: 'The fool says in his heart, "There is no God."' What is a fool in Bible language? It is a person without knowledge. It does not mean a person with a low IQ. It means someone who is ignorant of fact. The fool should, or could, know there is a God but chooses to reject the obvious. 'In his heart' shows that the denial of the existence of God is wilful and is not a flight of fancy, or something coming out of desperation, frustration or anger. No, the belief that there is no God runs deep.

The psalmist notes the reason for this inability or unwillingness to look at truth. The verse continues: 'They are corrupt, they do abominable deeds, there is none that does good.' Moral, spiritual and theological corruption is the problem, rather than an analysis of fact. The corruptness of the human heart is the source of the ignorance. There is also the idea that a corrupt person will simply not want to cease from wrongdoing — the expectation if you acknowledge the existence of the holy God of the Bible. Jesus said much the same thing in John 3:19–20: 'And this is the judgement, that the light has come into the world, and men loved darkness rather than light, because their deeds were evil. For every one who does evil hates the light, and does not come to the light, lest his deeds should be exposed.'

A second reason for rejecting life beyond the grave, one that springs naturally from the John 3 passage above, is that our deeds are evil and we are therefore fearful of being found out. What bigger exposure can there be than judgement before a holy and righteous God who has the right to judge because he is our Creator? People are strongly tempted to rely on theories that postulate that the grave is the end and cling to these theories simply out of fear that they may have to face up to their sinful ways.

I remember how it was before I became a Christian. I knew some things about Christianity. I had been to church with my dad, before I was big enough to resist. Although I was an unbeliever, I had a sense that somehow I was not going to be able to get away with all the things I had done. I did not talk to anyone about this and I did not dwell on it in my mind because it was unpleasant to think about. God puts a sense of judgement into us — into our conscience. Paul seems to indicate this very fact in Romans 1:18–19: 'For the wrath of God is revealed from heaven against all ungodliness and wickedness of men who by their wickedness suppress the truth. For what can be known about God is plain to them, because God has shown it to them.'

A third reason why the idea that the grave is the end is attractive is that it seems to provide liberty and freedom. Frank Sinatra sang, 'I did it my way.' I cannot help thinking that this meant the freedom to do whatever he wanted to do — including some things that he would not have wanted plastered all over the morning paper. Have you ever felt restrained or inhibited by laws and authorities? The rebellious mind protests, 'If I could just get rid of restraint! If I could be free of authority!' Such freedom-lovers feel that laws choke out their freedom and happiness: 'I'm not free to do what I want to do.'

The problem is, as long as there is a God, especially one who is righteous and holy, no one can be truly free to do whatever he or she wants without consequences, either immediate or ultimate. Personally, I know exactly what this feels like; I have been there. I know how it can anger, frustrate and even incite to rebellion. Yes, atheism comes naturally to those who want to sin and want to get away with it.

The fourth reason for gambling that the grave is the end is an abhorrence of the notion that there is a hell. And you do not need to be an atheist to believe this one.

Some find the evidence for a Creator to be very strong. For instance, the information/programmer argument is very compelling. We have learned that our DNA is coded with a huge amount of information. From computer science we recognize that stored information requires a programmer and something as complex as life requires an *amazing* programmer. Also persuasive is that the material for the universe had to come from somewhere, probably from somebody. Because of these and other arguments, many people will admit that there is a God. Some will even accept much of what the Bible says about Jesus, but they will reject the doctrine of hell. It amounts, on an emotional level at any rate, to about the same as the doctrine that the grave is the end of it all. The point is simple: no God, no real penalty, no actual judgement and no accountability.

Let me make this direct appeal to you. If you gamble that there is no hell, do you really want to risk everything on something you cannot prove. Would you risk eternal life on your own negative, God-denying notion that the grave is the end? This is ultimate spiritual suicide. Please consider the words of Jesus in Matthew 25:46: 'And they will go away into eternal punishment, but the righteous into eternal life.'

There is a movement within Christianity, which is picking up momentum day by day, that is designed to avoid the horror of the biblical doctrine of hell. There is a revival of the concept of purgatory, a non-biblical concept that most associate with Roman Catholicism. It teaches that after death there will be an opportunity to work things out, avoid hell and eventually get to heaven. Some in the evangelical Christian camp are now embracing this doctrine. There is also the idea circulating that hell is nothing more than eternal death (annihilation) — virtually the same idea that the grave is the end. Several Christian-based cults already teach this concept.

I know that Christians, including preachers, like anyone else, want to be liked, accepted and approved. What an apparent advantage it would be for me if I would simply drop the notion that there is an eternal hell! If the Bible gave me the opportunity to get out of it, I would — you would never hear me talk about it. I am sorry that I have to speak of hell, but I must because the Bible clearly teaches it. Let me say, almost parenthetically, that the *popular* concept of hell that is often depicted in the comic strips, with demons, flames, pitchforks and so on, is not accurate — this view of hell, inspired by Dante, is overblown. We need to get a biblical view of hell directly from the Scriptures.

I am reminded of the parable of the rich man and Lazarus from Luke 16. Jesus told the story of someone who had died, yet was conscious and in torment in hell. It revolts us. We do not understand it, but dare we reject it because it is unpleasant? What will you do? The truth is that one day you will discover your error.

I have a cartoon from the morning paper. It reads: 'What do the dead atheist, the agnostic, and the saint have in common?' The answer is that they all know there is a God. But some will discover this too late. Hell can be a truth learned too late.

## The very worst case

The person who says the grave is the end not only remains deceived but she or he will deceive others. We do not live our lives in isolation. What I hold as true and precious, I communicate to those around me — to my children, my friends, other family members, to many people that I associate with; whatever I believe I communicate. I will not go into length about the story

Jesus told of 'one of these little ones' (Matt. 18:5–6), but he said it would be better for people who misled innocent ones that a millstone was hung around their neck and they were dropped into the sea. This parable employs an idiom that is not to be taken literally, but Jesus taught that to be engaged in the process of deceiving others is a very serious thing. If you believe that the grave is the end not only have you been duped, but you are no doubt duping others.

## A protest

Someone might protest: 'You are using fear as a tactic to convince me to believe in Jesus.' If I could do that, I probably would try. However, no one can scare you into the kingdom of God. Oh, I may frighten you; I may cause you to rethink your position. I may cause you to come to the place where you reason, 'Well, I'd better take another look at this.' But I cannot scare you into the kingdom of God. Faith and trust in Jesus are a gift that comes by the power of the Holy Spirit. Jesus taught that we must be born again before we can enter the kingdom of heaven.

You cannot be scared into the kingdom of heaven, but maybe I can persuade you to look at Jesus afresh today. That is what I invite you to do, to see in Jesus the crucified and risen Saviour. I also must warn you of your danger. What doctor, after examining a patient and discovering a disease, will not warn of the danger? What physician would ignore that and say, 'Go home. You are all right. See you next year,' when he knows a disease is raging? For those who hope the grave is the end, you have a spiritual disease that will ultimately lead to a terrible eternity. Therefore, I must say, by the love of God, turn to Jesus. Why should you live your life basing all that you have and are on a gamble that you are sure to lose?

# CHAPTER 3

# You have been duped if you think God must be fair

This book is intentionally confrontational. I encourage you to challenge yourself to rethink your basic beliefs — or lack of beliefs — about God. The fact is, we have all been duped and no one more so than myself.

During the preparation of this book, I had to examine myself and acknowledge the ways I have been duped. If I were to feel the full impact of what I uncovered, I suspect it would be quite crushing. In the light of such a reality, I am comforted by these words of Jesus: 'Father, forgive them; for they know not what they do' (Luke 23:34). Though I did not know what I was doing, I was still headed in the wrong direction. My hands are not clean and neither are yours, but by God's grace we can face our delusions.

## Two illustrations: convicts and cultists

Not recognizing that we can be duped is dangerous; it is a sign of pride as well. Perhaps the following two illustrations will highlight my point.

'Duped' means 'deceived'; it means 'conned'. Over the last couple of decades, as a volunteer at San Quentin Prison, I have been conned many times. It is not that I have not known better. Twice a year, I sit through orientation and training sessions run by experts on the shenanigans that convicts get up to. The fact is that convicts are excellent at conning volunteers. It would be embarrassing for me to relate to you some of the ways I have been fooled. Some volunteers think that they are above deception and scoff at these sessions, which can be long and boring. Sadly, those who think they are above it all will sometimes have their volunteer privileges revoked due to misconduct — some have even gone to jail themselves.

Could you ever be caught up in a cult? Experts in the field of cults acknowledge that the person most vulnerable to cultic deception is the person who says, 'I'll never be duped by a cult.' For six years, in the 1980s, I facilitated a cult-recovery support group. Almost all the participants, as they came to terms with what had happened, expressed surprise that they could have been so tricked. To protect ourselves from cults, it is helpful to admit we are vulnerable — that is always the safest stance and it may serve us here as well.

## The fairness doctrine explained

The issue before us is what I call the 'fairness doctrine'. I call it a doctrine because it involves faith. You will not find the term in a dictionary or in a book of theological terms. It is a term that is used to describe an idea that has been around for a long time. Basically, it is a demand that God must be fair and that his decrees or principles must be reasonable and compatible with our human understanding of right and wrong. It holds God to a standard that we consider fair. Or, to put it another way, it is the creature judging the Creator.

In our good moments, we have a sense of fairness about us. In our most generous moments, we have a certain idea of how life should work. We are quick to say, 'That is not fair.' The problem comes when we suppose God must be fair according to how we view life.

One difference between youthful idealism and a more adult maturity is the acceptance of the fact that life is not fair. We learn that you can play the game, obey the rules, pay your taxes, do this good thing, avoid that bad thing, and yet bad things still happen.

We were recently hit with the news that a woman in our church family has cancer. And we ask 'Why?' Here is a gentle, loving person who has lived a clean life, never smoked, shopped almost exclusively at health-food stores, exercised regularly, and yet comes down with a life-threatening disease. She now faces invasive surgery and weeks of radiation and chemotherapy. We all know of such things — and saints do suffer.

There is no guarantee that if we are honest, brave and upright, life is necessarily going to go well. Indeed, youthful idealism will be shattered as we grow up. Despite this learning experience, many hold on to the idea that God is the great-granddaddy in the sky, a fairy godmother that should make everything right with the touch of a magic wand. So it is that when we bend God to the shape we desire, inadvertently, unconsciously even, we create a god in our image.

## God in our image

We would like God to be how we want him to be. We who are dead in our trespasses and sins, deceived and corrupted, desire to embrace a God with whom we are comfortable. Remember what the prophet Jeremiah said: 'The heart is deceitful above all things, and desperately corrupt...' (Jer. 17:9). In that state we create a God who will approve us, who will excuse us, who will not judge sin and who will save us all in the end.

Even in evangelical Christianity, efforts are made to avoid unpleasant doctrines. For instance, there is an attempt to reject or soften the doctrine of hell, as discussed in the previous chapter. We are busy developing theologies we are comfortable with, and the fairness doctrine definitely fits into the category.

## Jesus confronted the duped

Jesus directly confronted people who had been duped. Jesus attempted to reach out to those who had been theologically deceived, and that is what I am hoping to do as well. I am not here to point the finger. Someone who has been duped as much as I have cannot point a finger at anyone. The desire of Jesus was not to put people down or to cast blame upon them, but to help them see their error and to heal their blindness. And that is my interest. I wish that someone had done that for me in my theological confusion.

Dr Fred Fisher, late professor of New Testament and Greek at Golden Gate Seminary, did make an effort to turn me around when I was operating with an incorrect view of the church. In 1968 he called me on the telephone. I had never talked to him before — I did not particularly like him or perhaps I was a little afraid of him. Anyway, I thought he was a bit of a character. He was also one of the most renowned Southern Baptist New Testament scholars at the time. He smoked cigars and I did not like him for that — I was a real purist then. All throughout the building, even in the chapel, you could smell Dr Fisher's cigar. He was a tough old man, very learned and an oft-published author; I still have a couple of his books on my shelf. He said he would like to talk with me so I visited him at the seminary. He said, 'Kent, you are wrong about two or three issues.' I did not accept his counsel at the time but later on I did — I lived to discover he had been entirely right. That was the one time in my life when someone said to me, 'Philpott, examine what you are doing.' I wish that more people had had the courage to confront me. But today we are too polite. Jesus was not too polite to confront those who had been theologically duped.

Let us consider what Jesus said to the crowds and to his disciples in Matthew 23:2–7:

> The scribes and the Pharisees sit on Moses' seat; so practise and observe whatever they tell you, but not what they do; for they preach, but do not practise. They bind heavy burdens, hard to bear, and lay them on men's shoulders; but they themselves will not move them with their finger. They do all their deeds to be seen by men; for they make their phylacteries broad and their fringes long, and they love the place of honour at feasts and the best seats in the synagogues, and salutations in the market places, and being called rabbi by men.

Jesus deliberately attacked theological error and the self-righteous stand that many of the religious leaders of his day took. He made a diligent and dangerous effort to reach out to others.

## A hard saying

The following text goes right to the centre of the conflict — to the doctrine against which the fairness doctrine is most often directed. Jesus said, 'Enter by the narrow gate; for the gate is wide and the way is easy, that leads to destruction, and those who enter by it are many. For the gate is narrow and the way is hard, that leads to life, and those who find it are few' (Matt. 7:13–14).

Many Christians, as well as non-Christians, would like to highlight this passage and hit the delete key. Why? 'Narrow', 'hard' and 'few'. The fairness doctrine demands 'wide', 'easy' and 'many'. And would you not prefer the broadly inclusive terms too? Some are bewildered by what Jesus said; others are angered.

And it seems to get worse. These verses come later in the chapter:

> Not every one who says to me, 'Lord, Lord,' shall enter the kingdom of heaven, but he who does the will of my Father who is in heaven.

On that day many will say to me, 'Lord, Lord, did we not prophesy in your name, and cast out demons in your name, and do many mighty works in your name?' And then will I declare to them, 'I never knew you; depart from me, you evildoers' (Matt. 7:21–23).

Jesus is focusing on religious people. He is not content with pointing out the extreme danger of the irreligious and now warns the religious types, the spiritual people who think they are in God's inner circle. They are the ones saying, 'Lord, Lord.' Who would be saying such things except religious, spiritual people?

'That day', Jesus said. Do you know what day that is? Whenever you see 'that day' or a similar expression in the Bible it is referring to the Day of Judgement. On the Day of Judgement many will say, 'Lord, Lord.' The word 'Lord' is repeated, showing the fervent religiosity of the speakers. 'Did we not prophesy in your name?' That means, preach and proclaim as though God were actually speaking. And 'cast out demons in your name' — how many are engaged in this sort of thing? And 'do many mighty works in your name'. Could this refer to those who suppose they have the power to do signs and wonders? And Jesus will say to them all, 'I never knew you; depart from me, you evildoers.' This is the strongest possible warning. Jesus is speaking to those who had been deceived into thinking that their made-up religious ideas and rituals assured them of a place in heaven.

It is not preaching or casting out of demons that is the problem. There are some differences among Christians on these points. But everything has a counterfeit — including gospel preaching — and this fact has been frequently observed throughout the course of church history. There are false gospels, incomplete gospels and there are phony, even demonic, workings of miracles and castings out of demons. Jesus did not expand further, but the one thing that is apparent is that religiosity is no guarantee of divine approval.

## The exclusive claims

At the heart of our difficulty with the fairness doctrine are the exclusive claims of Jesus. Dozens of passages could be cited. Consider John 14:6: 'Jesus said to him, "I am the way, and the truth, and the life; no one comes to the Father, but by me."' Not only will there be few who will find safe haven and salvation, but it is *only through Jesus*. Obviously this does not sit well with the 'all roads lead to God' mentality. What about the Hindus, the Buddhists or the Muslims? That is why many protest: 'This is not fair!' And, we must admit, it does not seem fair from our human vantage point.

It is easy to see where the fairness doctrine comes from. We do not like to preach that few are going to find the narrow gate. We would like to reverse it and say, 'Almost everybody, except truly evil people like Hitler or Stalin, will ultimately be okay.' We would like to say that everyone who worships whatever god or goddess, everyone who is spiritual or religious, or tries hard and is sincere, will be safe too.

Bible-oriented Christians desire that *all* people should be forgiven and have eternal life. We want to be kind, accepting and generous, so much so that we can be tempted to adopt a more liberal position — to have a 'wider mercy' as some call it. We may find ourselves tempted to embrace a doctrine that teaches that many will find eternal happiness in heaven and that few, if any, are on the way to destruction and hell.

## Another view

Do not think that this present generation of Christians is the first that was ever tempted by or deceived by the fairness doctrine; it has been around for a long time. Paul deals with it directly in the ninth chapter of his letter to the church at Rome, written about A.D. 57. He writes of the time of the patriarchs, as recorded in Genesis, and specifically about Isaac and Rebecca and the birth of their twin sons, Jacob and Esau. The way things were in the culture of their day, the elder — even if older by only a minute — inherited the principal wealth, amounting to two-thirds or more of the patriarchal blessing. But it was not Esau, the first-born, who received Isaac's inheritance. Both materially and spiritually, Jacob did. Paul's point is that the selection of Jacob over Esau had nothing to do with fairness, as humans perceive it; it had all to do with God's will.

Paul continues: 'What shall we say then? Is there injustice on God's part?' (Rom. 9:14) Just as God had chosen the nation of Israel (not for any good in them), just as he had chosen Jacob and not Esau, so God has freely elected sinners to salvation — God has predestinated and chosen certain people. The natural objection arises that this is unjust. It came up in Paul's day and it comes up in our own. But Paul anticipated these objections and he continues: 'What shall we say then? Is there injustice on God's part? By no means! For he says to Moses, "I will have mercy on whom I have mercy, and I will have compassion on whom I have compassion"' (Rom. 9:14–15).

Examine your own feelings — does that truth upset you? It used to upset me a great deal. Often, when I considered election, I had to ask myself, 'Philpott, can you preach that legitimately? Do you think it is true?' But as I look at the Scriptures, I cannot find any alternative that is consistent with what is clearly revealed. On a purely human level, I would abandon this truth if I could. However, God says, 'I will have mercy on whom I will have mercy, and I will have compassion on whom I will have compassion.' Thus in our objections to God's stated intentions we find the origin of the fairness doctrine. We judge God and we say, 'God is not just. God is not fair.'

## The mercy of God

Consider Romans 9:16: 'So it depends not upon man's will or exertion, but upon God's mercy.' Once you see it is God's *mercy*, it changes for you. We are all lost and dead in our trespasses and sins. But God, in the midst of our horrendous rebellion, reaches out and, as John Wesley said, 'plucks the brand from the burning'.

Paul's argument continues: 'So then [God] has mercy upon whomever he wills, and he hardens the heart of whomever he wills' (Rom. 9:18). This does not seem fair, but election is the doctrine of *grace* (unmerited favour). Election is our hope of heaven since we are not able to save ourselves. We are not in charge. Either God rescues us, or we are lost.

Paul is not finished with his argument. He knows the trouble that arises when the doctrine of election is presented. 'You will say to me then, "Why does he still find fault? For who can resist his will?"' (Rom. 9:19). Does this sound like your response? 'But who are you, a man, to answer back to God? Will what is moulded say to its moulder, "Why have you made me thus?" Has the potter no right over the clay, to make out of the same lump one vessel for beauty and another for menial use?' (Rom. 9:20–21).

It is essential that we understand that God is the Creator, the Maker of heaven and earth. We must see that we are the creatures, and not only that, but also that we are flawed, to say the least. Human history and our own sense of inner pollution must teach us this. Yes, we are capable of the highest ideals and sentiments and may perform altruistic acts, but we know our own hearts. How arrogant of us to hold God to *our* standard of fairness!

I realize I am not going to be able to satisfy you on the fairness doctrine by asserting God's sovereignty, at least not on an emotional level. But I may be able to reach you on an intellectual level, which is a good start. It may take a long time for you to come to the point where you are completely able to accept the fairness of God. You must come to the place where you see that God is God and you cannot make him what you want him to be — otherwise you end up with an idol. And no idol saves.

## The fairness of God

The next verse to consider regarding the fairness of God is from the apostle John's first of three short letters found towards the end of the New Testament, written about A.D. 96. 'This is love: not that we loved God, but that he loved us and sent his Son as an atoning sacrifice for our sins' (1 John 4:10, NIV). Now what does 'atoning sacrifice' mean? It means that Jesus died in our place, thus atoning for (or covering) our sin. It means that he took our judgement, sin and hell upon himself because he loves us. In mercy God, in the person of his Son, rescued us.

The problem is always sin. My view is that the most important truth about God is that he is holy and just. To put it simply — no sin can come before God. If we, as he desires, are to spend eternity in his presence, then something must be done about our sin. We have sinned, and who among us would deny it?

What we cannot do (save or forgive ourselves), the Father accomplished in the sacrificial death of his Son, the Lord Jesus. On the cross, the Son bore our sin upon himself. His shed blood removed the *just penalty* of our sin. Therefore, we can now enter into the Father's presence. The whole ministry of the church is, and must be, the proclamation that in Christ our sin is forgiven. You see, it is not a question of fairness, it is a question of sin.

## Summary and conclusion

You have been duped if you think that the God of the Bible, in whom faithful Christians trust, must conform to your notion of fairness. Or, you have been duped if you reject the gospel of Christ because it appears to go against your own idea of fairness.

The Old Testament prophet Isaiah wrote, 'For as the heavens are higher than the earth, so are my ways higher than your ways and my thoughts than your thoughts' (Isa. 55:9). The Maker of heaven and earth, who spoke the universe into being, is greater than we are. Let the Potter fashion the clay as he would.

Some say, 'It would not be fair if God did not choose me.' Is the fear of not being chosen by God behind the fairness doctrine? I understand such a fear, but it is a fear based on ignorance of what Jesus and the cross are all about. Jesus said to enter in at the narrow gate. He said to come to him and anyone who came to him he would not cast out or reject. We are told, 'Believe in the Lord Jesus Christ, and you will be saved' (Acts 16:31). We are invited to 'Turn to [God] and be saved' (Isa. 45:22). God's electing grace will always be mysterious to us, but he is ready to forgive us and give us the gift of eternal life. So I say to you who believe in the fairness doctrine because you are afraid that God did not choose you, 'Trust in Jesus. Come to him. Believe in the Lord Jesus Christ and you will be safe.'

# CHAPTER 4

# You have been duped if you think all that matters is your happiness

What do you think of the title of this chapter? Are you angry or frustrated by it? More importantly, do you think this statement applies to you?

Some of you are part of the 'Me Generation' — hardly a flattering term. If you are among that generation by virtue of your year of birth, you are supposedly self-centred and self-absorbed. (I reject the stereotype since that characterizes *every* generation.) Maybe you will claim the distinction; maybe you will disown it. I am not of that generation, but it is still true of me. Is it true of you?

The American Declaration of Independence declares the right to 'life, liberty, and the pursuit of happiness'. Is happiness a birthright in America? Happiness is not guaranteed, rather the right to pursue it. Today many people think that finding happiness is the whole point of life.

Sometimes it seems that the universal complaint is: 'I'm not happy!' This implies that you should be happy. This is not likely to be the sentiment of those living on the edge of existence in the Third World, but it is often true of us here in the West. We look around for someone or some circumstance to blame when things do not go our way. Parents are often blamed; sometimes it is the government, or the schools, or something outside of us, or out of our control. How easily we make ourselves victims when we are unhappy and dissatisfied! Time and again people complain, 'I have a right to be happy and if I am not happy, something is wrong.' I would like to challenge that idea because you have been duped if you think the goal of your life is personal happiness.

## Jesus confronted the duped

Once again, let us observe how Jesus himself dealt with this issue. Matthew 23 records the story of a confrontation Jesus had with the religious leaders of his day. He says:

> But woe to you, scribes and Pharisees, hypocrites! because you shut the kingdom of heaven against men; for you neither enter yourselves, nor allow those who would enter to go in. Woe to you, scribes and Pharisees, hypocrites! for you traverse sea and land to make a single proselyte, and when he becomes a proselyte, you make him twice as much a child of hell as yourselves (Matt. 23:13–15).

Can you imagine how this would have struck these men? How would you feel if someone spoke to you in such a way? Jesus had the courage to challenge error. People then, as now, were locked into their viewpoints. Jesus was hoping to tear down that he might build up. Jesus was showing them the seriousness of their distortion of truth so that they would confront their own error.

## Strong preaching

When you examine the preaching that has preceded great, powerful revivals and awakenings, you will see that it is characterized by a clear and strong proclamation of Jesus and the cross. So it was with the French reformer, John Calvin. Writing from Geneva, in the sixteenth century, Calvin noted that strong preaching preceded the European awakenings. In the eighteenth century, the time of the First Great Awakening in America, the courageous preaching of Jonathan Edwards, Gilbert Tennent, John Wesley, Samuel Davies and George Whitefield stood out. Then there were the powerful, jarring sermons of Timothy Dwight in the early nineteenth century. He was president of Yale College, a school for training ministers. It had slipped into rank decay and Dwight, the grandson of Jonathan Edwards, challenged his students: 'You have come to study in a university to prepare you for the ministry, and you are not even converted yourselves. You have no godliness and no spirituality. You do not pray. You do not read your Bible' (paraphrase by the author). Such strong, fearless preaching fanned into flame the Second Great Awakening. Dwight confronted the students in sermon after sermon until finally only a few would come to the chapel services. But, one by one, the students who were coming to chapel began to be converted. Soon, almost the entire seminary was converted and the Second Great Awakening was underway. If Timothy Dwight had stopped preaching because of the unfavourable reaction of the students there might have been no awakening, at least not at Yale.

If Jesus had not confronted some of the scribes and the Pharisees, perhaps the esteemed leader of Judaism, Nicodemus, would not have been converted. Or perhaps another Pharisee, the rich religious leader Joseph of Arimathea, would not have been either. But Jesus had their highest interest in mind. He was not merely interested in making their present life happy and prosperous. He knew they would one day die and then face judgement. If he had given them all they wanted in this life, they would no doubt have achieved some happiness. But what is that — a few years — in the face of eternity? Jesus reached out to people whatever their current condition. He wanted to stir up the complacent and he used confrontational language to do so. It may be that you will experience the same here, and to the same end.

## A lesson from a seeker of happiness

Consider King Solomon of Israel. He was the son of David and Bathsheba, and was a man noted for his wisdom. He sought personal happiness diligently. Here is his testimony, from Ecclesiastes 2:1–11:

> I said to myself, 'Come now, I will make a test of pleasure; enjoy yourself.' But behold, this also was vanity. I said of laughter, 'It is mad,' and of pleasure, 'What use is it?' I searched with my mind how to cheer my body with wine — my mind still guiding me with wisdom — and how to lay hold on folly, till I might see what was good for the sons of men to do under heaven during the few days of their life. I made great works; I built houses and planted vineyards for myself; I made myself gardens and parks, and planted in them all kinds of fruit trees. I made myself pools from which to water the forest of growing trees. I bought male and female slaves, and had slaves who were born in my house; I had also great possessions of herds and flocks, more than any who had been before me in Jerusalem. I also gathered for myself silver and gold and the treasure of kings and provinces; I got singers, both men and women, and many concubines, man's delight.

So I became great and surpassed all who were before me in Jerusalem; also my wisdom remained with me. And whatever my eyes desired I did not keep from them; I kept my heart from no pleasure, for my heart found pleasure in all my toil, and this was my reward for all my toil. Then I considered all that my hands had done and the toil I had spent in doing it, and behold, all was vanity and a striving after wind, and there was nothing to be gained under the sun.

And then in verse 17 of that same chapter he writes, 'So I hated life, because what is done under the sun was grievous to me; for all is vanity and a striving after wind.'

Solomon ended up hating life. And I have found the same with those who thought their happiness was all that mattered. Have you ever wondered, 'Why do people get so grumpy as they get older?' I think one reason for it is that those who focus on satisfying themselves become frustrated and desperate — they end up cynical and grumpy.

Here is another statement from Solomon: 'And I thought the dead who are already dead more fortunate than the living who are still alive; but better than both is he who has not yet been, and has not seen the evil deeds that are done under the sun' (Eccles. 4:2–3). Solomon came to the same conclusion that anyone will who thinks that the chief goal of life is attaining personal happiness. You might now protest, 'You mean I am supposed to be unhappy? Is the goal of my life to be unhappy?'

## To be happy or not

Although Solomon had tried hard to enjoy life, he had a rather negative view of his life and the despair that pleasure-seeking brought him. Jesus, however, had a different sense of life — in our primary text, John 10:10, Jesus affirmed an 'abundant' life. There is clear biblical support that we are not on the planet to live miserably!

In the early verses of John 10, Jesus referred to himself as the door of the sheepfold and the Good Shepherd. In those days, sheep ranching was a major industry. A sheepfold was usually an area around which a low stone wall had been built and into which there was one narrow entrance. The shepherd was on guard day and night to protect the sheep. There were sheep-stealers, both human and animal, and Jesus speaks of them in verse 10: 'The thief comes only to steal and kill and destroy.'

'Thief' is probably a metaphor. We might guess that the thief is Satan, but Jesus does not make any specific identification. The thief might be a false teacher, or anyone who would make a deliberate effort to turn someone away from Jesus — even a close friend or a family member. Probably, however, the thief refers to any number of ideas, or systems of ideas, which turn someone away from Christ.

What truly moves or motivates people, tribes or nations? 'Ideas', is my answer. Things that we believe in and have committed ourselves to — these things energize and even control our lives. An enemy's most advanced weapon comes in the form of an idea, and this is especially true when it comes to the only significant facet of life — knowing and having fellowship with the Creator God. Jesus said, 'The thief comes to steal, kill, and destroy.'

In the second part of the verse 10, Jesus said, 'I came that they may have life, and have it abundantly.' The contrast is beyond our ability to measure. Life and death are poles apart and when you consider that it is a question of *eternal* life and death, you begin to appreciate the magnitude of the difference. I would like to emphasize this last point. The life that Jesus is speaking of has a dual dimension to it. It is life *now* as well as life in the *future*. Jesus clearly means that those who are in the sheepfold (those who belong to him and look to him as the Good Shepherd) have abundant life *right now*. We do not want necessarily to equate abundant life with happiness. A person can be happy, characteristically or temporarily, but not have abundant life. A person can have the abundant life Jesus gives and be unhappy. Happiness is a detail.

As soon as I say this, I realize that God is also interested in our happiness, but happiness in a way not ordinarily assumed by most people. Remember, Jesus said, 'I am the way, and the truth, and the life' (John 14:6). This is one of the verses mentioned in the previous chapter about the so-called fairness doctrine, and it is a claim that many detest. It is an exclusive declaration. But the point I want to make is that Jesus is *himself* 'life'. To miss this is to miss everything. The life lived in fellowship with Jesus, life filled with the Holy Spirit, life that will never end, useful, complete, fulfilled — this is life. It is life fuller than that lived by Adam and Eve in the Garden of Eden. It is abundant life now.

Does living an abundant life also mean living a happy life? Perhaps, but not necessarily, and I emphasize this point so as to avoid confusion. True happiness is found in knowing Jesus. Paul, in speaking of the gifts of the

Holy Spirit, taught that we are growing up 'to the measure of the stature of the fulness of Christ' (Eph. 4:13). Therefore, the Christian life is one of discovery and that makes for a life of adventure and excitement. This 'knowing' is gradual and constant, and is worked in us by the Holy Spirit. It is a spiritual nurturing and is based on knowledge of the Scripture, prayer, worship, service and fellowship in the church.

Jesus is always more than we know at any one point because he keeps on revealing himself to us. As he said in John 14:21, 'He who loves me will be loved by my Father, and I will love him and *manifest* myself to him.' Jesus is the Alpha and the Omega, the beginning and the end, but we are from the dust — it will take an eternity for us to discover the depths and riches of his person. This is part of the wonder of being in Christ.

## Getting personal

At this moment, I am not particularly happy. I am fairly miserable — but I have Jesus, and that makes all the difference. Despite my current state, I know that he loves me, has forgiven me, has given me a job and a vision for the future that I cherish, and one day, either by my death or his return, he will receive me into his presence for ever. I may be temporarily unhappy; nevertheless, I have a real sense of abundant life, and my sense of 'happiness' will return.

## Beyond happiness

Christians have a rich and extensive library in the recorded experiences of spiritual brothers and sisters from the early church. In this library are stories both of glory and suffering. In the very first volume, we encounter Jesus, the Lord of glory, who lived a short, difficult life, full of grief and pain. He was betrayed, abandoned, unfairly tried and cruelly executed as a common criminal. All but one of the apostles, died a violent death. There have been thousands upon thousands of martyrs over the long centuries since then. Yet these men and women attest that to die for Christ is gain (Phil. 1:21). And, as a pastor with more than three decades of experience, I attest that the ordinary Christian is no different. Despite what life may bring, the abundant life in Christ Jesus is tangible.

The abundant life is beyond happiness. It may include happiness but it is more than that. It is love, peace and joy in the Holy Spirit. It is walking in fellowship with God. It is serving the true and the living God. It is confidence in our eternal security. It is learning to know God through his Word and in prayer. It is knowing that our sins are forgiven and our guilt is removed. It is life, work and fellowship in his body, the church. It is a life of great adventure and challenge. It is beyond description and it is definitely more than just happiness.

Jesus taught that those who lose their life would find it and those who find their life would lose it (John 12:25). This is a great paradox, powerful in its contradiction, but I think Jesus had in mind the same point that I am dealing with. If the pursuit of happiness is all that matters to us, we lose that which is actually of greatest value.

## A happy Margaret Hastings

In the October 2001 edition of the *Evangelical Times*, Faith Cook wrote an article on Selina Hastings, the Countess of Huntingdon. Born in England in 1707, Selina became a friend and sponsor of John and Charles Wesley, George Whitefield and other notable English preachers during the First Great Awakening. Selina was greatly influenced by the statement her sister-in-law Margaret Hastings made some time after her own conversion: 'Since I have known the Lord Jesus Christ for salvation, I have been as happy as an angel.' Margaret's statement had a great impact on the unhappy and often fearful Selina and some time later she trusted in Jesus as her Saviour. Selina later testified how her sister-in-law's testimony had been so influential in her conversion.

Margaret Hastings had found happiness in Jesus, and so did Selina, but it was not happiness that Margaret and Selina sought — it was the Saviour, Jesus Christ.

## Happiness — temporary and unfulfilling

Do not suppose that I am saying that anyone outside of Jesus cannot be happy! I look back on my life before I was a Christian and I remember that I was not a particularly unhappy person. I naturally have a personality that is upbeat and optimistic and I enjoyed whatever I did. But there is a deeper happiness to be found in Christ. This abundant life is sometimes spoken of as joy and peace; it is sometimes spoken of as love. If we think we have been born to be happy and that is what we are owed, we will become cynical complainers because life usually does not turn out that way.

We must remember that we are soul and spirit. We are spiritual because we are created in the image of God. As the early Church Father Augustine wrote, 'Our heart is restless, until it rest in thee.' God made us so we would be restless until we rest in him, and no amount of so-called happiness will suffice.

## The entertainment industry

We live in a world that is frequently an unhappy one. The 'pink' section of the *San Francisco Sunday Chronicle* vividly illustrates our lust for entertainment and distraction. The enormous effort and money that goes into entertainment is staggering. What a huge industry it is too — film, TV, sports, theatre, music, gambling, travel, pornography, and much more! It is probably the most expansive business on the planet. Certainly, many of us enjoy art, music, laughter, and so on. Entertainment is not wrong in and of itself. People who know me realize what a sports fan I am; I also enjoy art, music, drama, television and film. But I find, as you may, that such 'happiness' is fleeting at best.

And then there are myriads of products that promise to enhance our lives or dull the jagged edges of our existence, even if for just a little while. This is essentially the peddling of images that promise happiness, power, prestige, love, wealth, sex, and so on. Promoters entice us with lines like: 'If you buy this product, you are going to…' It is an unhappy world and we are easily enticed — and the major product we think we are buying is happiness. 'Life, liberty, and the pursuit of happiness,' America's founding fathers wrote.

## The contrast

In contrast to the empty promises to provide happiness of human invention, Jesus is the bread of life that truly satisfies. He said, 'I am the bread of life' (John 6:48). He is the living water that quenches our thirst. He said, 'If any one thirst, let him come to me and drink' (John 7:37). He alone satisfies our hunger. He alone quenches our thirst. He is the one who brings life.

Consider Paul's words in Ephesians 1:12: 'We who first hoped in Christ have been destined and appointed to live for the praise of his glory.' Paul does not say that we have been destined and appointed to be happy, or that the essence of our living is to be a quest to find happiness. Once the reality of this verse becomes a part of our lives, it changes everything. Happiness, at least, is placed in perspective. We may find happiness, or we may not; this is not the issue. If we do find happiness in living for the praise of God's glory, it is a by-product of living for and with Jesus. We are more likely to find happiness when we are not looking for it. We will be 'surprised by joy', as C. S. Lewis, the renowned English scholar and author, described his conversion.

## Who benefits from this sort of living?

Is living to the 'praise of his glory' good for God, or good for us? How do you answer this question? Some of you will say it is for our good, some of you will say God's, and some will say both. When I live to honour my Creator and lift him up, I am living how God intended that I should live. To exalt the name of Jesus — this is God's intent and his purpose for me. After all, Jesus' name is above every name, and at his name every knee shall bow (Phil. 2:9–11). To live to honour and praise my Lord Jesus is the very best for me, and results in my greatest benefit.

Consider also that *God delights in us*. He made us for himself. No parent is happy when a child is in trouble, and so it is with our heavenly Father. He loves us and wants us to love him. So, when we live for the praise of his glory, it pleases God and brings *him* joy.

## The corruption of happiness

Sin has tremendous power. It dulls our pleasure. Sin prevents us from experiencing an enjoyable, abundant life. Because God is interested in our well-being, he sent his only Son to atone for our sin. He provided the sacrifice for sin that we might be forgiven. Jesus substituted himself in our place. This is the core of the gospel — the atoning or covering work that takes away our sin. The terrible blight of sin does not have to control and frustrate our lives. Remember, the pleasures of sin last only a short time and, compared to eternity, what is that?

## Summary

We are to glorify, praise and worship God. This should be the primary goal of our life. Whether our life is long or short, whether peaceful and tranquil or stressful and chaotic, whether wonderful or somewhat less than wonder-ful, even miserable by the world's standards — these characterizations are essentially irrelevant. Living for the praise of the glory of God proves to be the best kind of living.

Our Maker does not guarantee a long, peaceful and healthy life. He does not guarantee a short, miserable one, either. But our life is the life that we have, and each life is important and potentially meaningful.

Every life is somewhat different. Some outwardly experience more of the fruit of living in terms of material wealth, health, human love or friendship, or longevity. These are mere details when viewed from the perspective of eternity; they are not the central issues of our life. Our primary goal is to live for the praise of his glory — this is what we are about. We are more than clay and genes. We are made in the image of God and to know him personally and live to honour him is the highest calling.

If you have been duped into thinking that the goal of your life is to find happiness, you will probably find just enough of it to keep you searching for more. Every once in a while, you will experience a little bit of happiness but it will be temporary, fleeting and will not satisfy in the long term.

## A closing reflection

There may not be a greater deception than to believe that the goal of our life is to be happy. You may yet change your mind, embrace another view, and be delivered from the cynicism and despair that comes from an all-out seeking of your own happiness. Heed the wisdom of King Solomon — live for Jesus instead.

# CHAPTER 5

# You have been duped if you are convinced that whatever you believe must be true

The dominant characteristic of our age is relativism. Simply put, this means, 'Whatever you believe must be true.' Relativism has some truth to it — there is a certain sense that a belief affects the believer and is then 'truth' for that believer. But what is 'true for you' may not be true at all.

## Post-postmodernism

Relativism is the hallmark of what is called postmodernism. Postmodernism has replaced modernism and will one day be replaced by post-postmodernism. Modernism, briefly, focused on human reason and was propelled by discoveries and developments in science and technology. This movement was helpful and liberating to a degree — it opened up possibilities and provided the freedom to think and explore. Modernism, however, bypassed God. Postmodernism takes this even further. In adding subjectivity (relativism), plurality (tolerance for all) and existentialism (feelings can dictate truth), the postmodern world-view is one in which truth is entirely personal and free of absolutes (subjective rather than objective).

The reason I think postmodernism is doomed is that relativism, however fashionable and politically correct now, is just plain nonsense — that is, unless all concern for what is true, right and real is abandoned. If the issue of truth does not actually matter and all things are equal — and the demand for moral and ethical freedom remains high — then relativism will continue to survive as a dominant paradigm. However, people do have a desire to make sense of their world and so, at some point, we may arrive at post-postmodernism when objective truth is valued once again.

## The impact of Darwinism on relativism

Relativism did not make its appearance in either the modern or postmodern period. It is an ancient philosophy most often held by practical atheists. The belief in a supreme and holy Deity imposes certain restraints on those bent on living out the urges of their fallen nature, but in the nineteenth century the impact of Darwin's theory of evolution made it easier to dispose of a Creator God altogether. Thus relativism, where everyone is right in his or her own eyes, gained acceptance and became widespread.

I am not going to argue the issues about evolution except to say that I accept micro-evolution (adaptation within a species) but I reject macro-evolution (the theory that everything evolved from a single life organism). The more I examine the issue, the more I believe macro-evolution is a huge leap of faith — the scientific evidence does not back it up. Evolution exists merely as a theory and not a fact. Despite that, those committed to macro-evolution will continue to believe in it unless their minds are opened to a 'Cause' that started it all. (For those wishing to pursue this matter further, let me recommend an excellent booklet: John Blanchard, *Evolution: Fact or Fiction?* Evangelical Press, September 2002.)

## Are you a relativist?

Suppose you do not like what I just said. You might think I am completely wrong and reject my thesis altogether. If so, you are not a relativist. You have the ability to think your own thoughts and say 'No!' — so much the better. But if you find it difficult to disagree because you would not want to offend me, or if you feel you must grant me my 'truth', then you are mired in relativistic thought.

## Do you find this offensive?

Are you offended by the idea that what you believe may not be true? Personally, I can say 'yes' to that. I admit I tend towards being arrogant and conceited and 'being wise in my own eyes'. I like to be right; I do not like to be challenged. However, to blindly embrace a philosophical concept like relativism is not prudent. To declare that truth is what I want it to be is to approach insanity. Will you have a greater interest in what is truth, has been truth from the beginning and will be truth for ever, than in protecting your closely-held beliefs? The issue is eternal life and death; you cannot afford to be misled.

## The Raelians

Don Lattin, religion editor of the *San Francisco Chronicle*, recently wrote about the Raelians (19 August 2001). Alongside the article was a picture of Brigitte Boisselier, a member of the Raelians and director of Clonaid. The Raelians are very much interested in human cloning. They are hoping to persuade the authorities to support research into human cloning and, I might add, attract media attention. Lattin wrote of Boisselier's efforts: 'Earlier this month, she single-handedly restored public confidence in the spiritual beliefs of those members of our society who happen to believe that God is a little green man who visited Planet Earth on a flying saucer.' We may laugh at Lattin's spoof, but for those who accept relativism, Boisselier's sincerity and firm conviction cannot easily be dismissed. Some people might even ask, 'Where can I find out about this wonderful group?'

Claude Vorilhon, a former French racecar driver and sports journalist, founded the Raelians in 1973. He is now known as Rael, or 'The Messenger'. He claims he was abducted by aliens and taken into a flying saucer where he received divine revelation. After a conversation with a four-foot-tall alien with a 'slightly greenish tinge', Vorilhon was never the same. The alien told him that humans had been created by superior beings through genetic engineering and advanced cloning techniques. Other things that supposedly happened on board the spaceship are even more incredible, but the problem is, how can such a claim be evaluated? After all, Vorilhon's 'truth' is truth for him.

In December 2002, Dr Boisselier announced that the Raelians had cloned humans. This has caused quite a reaction. The report, currently unverified, is apparently attracting converts to the movement. However wacky and weird the claim may be, some people will believe anything — they have lost their ability to discern truth from fiction.

## Truth for you

Lattin wrote the article in a tongue-in-cheek manner — he was apparently making sport of the Raelians. If you are a relativist, however, you cannot so easily dismiss such extreme points of view. We may poke fun at strange beliefs, but the relativist is ill-equipped to reject absurdities.

Many people have bought into the notion that if something is sincerely espoused it is truth, or becomes truth, for the believer. But if it is truth for you and I reject it, am I rejecting you too? This is difficult for those who desire to please and appease. One major problem with relativism is that it may preclude proper and prudent evaluation, at least public evaluation, lest some person or group be offended. This can be disastrous.

## The secular, cultural anthropological approach to religious truth

Cultural anthropologists examine the diversity of world-views and the human effort to make sense of life and death. They attempt to accurately record and describe, based on the accounts of adherents, the various belief systems without evaluation or prejudice. While it is a valuable pursuit and is not intended to promote relativism, in the popular mind it tends to do just that.

Belief systems help order individual and social life and are of intrinsic value to believers. But it is beyond the scientific purpose of the anthropologist to declare religious ideas right or wrong. The problem is that such a value-free approach to research and reporting contributes to the acceptance of relativism.

The study of comparative religions, in addition, is merely descriptive. Its purpose is not to make pronouncements as to the truth of the religion under study. And again, like cultural anthropology, while it is not an attempt to promote relativism, it does so nevertheless.

In general, people do not like to evaluate another person's religious beliefs negatively. They may therefore fall into the trap of relativism — whatever you believe must at least be respected if not regarded as truth. I am not espousing a curtailing or a denying of the freedom of religion or speech; I am upholding the need for critical evaluation.

Inherent in relativism is the understanding that there is no actual truth — no ultimate, almighty Deity, who *is* truth. If everything is true, then nothing is really true; it is only interesting cultural diversity. Religious beliefs are reduced to absurdity — quaint doctrines and practices that make for fascinating study.

## Jesus confronted error

Jesus attacked false doctrines that damaged people and kept them from the love and grace of a compassionate God. In some of the chapters of this book, I have selected a story from one of the Gospels where Jesus challenged people who had embraced lies. Here is another example. This one is from Matthew 23:23–24: 'Woe to you, scribes and Pharisees, hypocrites! for you tithe mint and dill and cummin, and have neglected the weightier matters of the law, justice and mercy and faith; these you ought to have done, without neglecting the others. You blind guides, straining out a gnat and swallowing a camel!'

Jesus began with, 'Woe to you.' I think if you were to have heard it in Aramaic, the language Jesus spoke, the phrase would have sounded like 'oy vay' — an expression I used as a kid growing up in Los Angeles. 'Woe to you' is strong language. Woe means that something very unpleasant is coming down the road for you.

The religious elite, the scribes and Pharisees, were the most educated people of their day — they were highly respected. Today the words 'Pharisee' and 'scribe' have a negative connotation, but not so in their day. They were much admired. To these learned and dignified leaders, Jesus said 'Woe to you!' They must have bristled upon hearing those words. He called them 'blind guides'; he said they strained out gnats but swallowed camels, which meant that their priorities were askew. Jesus wanted them to know they had been deceived and, consequently, would be deceiving others.

Why would Jesus speak like this to revered spiritual leaders? The answer, I am convinced, was to break down barriers. He wanted those who had unwittingly cloaked themselves in error to open their eyes and their ears that they might see who he really was. The doctrines they had embraced, like the doctrine of relativism in our own day, blinded them. This is why Jesus spoke as he did.

## The text: John 14:6

Our primary text is John 14:6: 'Jesus said to him, "I am the way, and the truth, and the life; no one comes to the Father, but by me."'

If you are committed to relativism and pluralism, your reaction might be: 'That is extremely narrow.' The clear intent of these words of Jesus would amount to a violation, technically, of the doctrine of relativism since Christ alone is presented as the only truth — but relativism will go only so far. This statement of Jesus, taken at face value, demands a choice. Either he is right or he is wrong. The relativist shrinks from being backed into a corner like this.

Notice, Jesus did not say, 'I am going to teach you the way. I am going to talk to you about life. I am going to speak to you about things that are true.' He did not say anything remotely like that. Rather he used the phrase 'I am,' which in Greek is the equivalent to the Hebrew word YHWH, the covenant name for the God of Israel. Jesus directly and clearly announced who he is. His hearers would have understood him to mean, 'I, who am God, I am the way. I am the truth. I am the life. I am not teaching you *about* the way and *about* the truth and *about* the life, I *am* life, I *am* truth, I *am* the way.' By 'way', Jesus means the way to God the Father, or the way to forgiveness and eternal life. No other founder of a major world religion ever spoke in these categorical terms.

Christians do not believe true things as much as we believe truth; that is, we believe in Jesus. The two are quite different. The sum and substance of Christianity is not a set of doctrines, though we do have creeds and doctrinal statements like the Apostles' Creed. We believe the Apostles' Creed expresses essential biblical truth. But believing the doctrines is secondary to believing in Jesus. Assent to doctrine *about* Jesus does not result in the new birth and forgiveness of sin; rather it is *faith in* Jesus himself and what he accomplished on the cross that brings peace with God.

## The Jesus Movement motto

Because Jesus is himself the way, the truth and the life, then it follows, as our text proclaims, that 'No one comes to the Father but by me.'

I was part of the Jesus Movement of the late 1960s and early 1970s. Our motto was 'One Way' and the sign of the movement was the index finger pointing up to heaven. Hippies, during the 1960s, used to flash the V sign (the peace sign that Winston Churchill made famous during World War II as the sign of victory) but in the Jesus Movement, the index finger pointing skyward was the sign. We were symbolizing that there was one way to God.

The reason the 'One Way' sign was so prominent in the Jesus Movement was that there had been a tremendous explosion in the acceptance and popularity of Eastern religious teachings. The Jesus Movement directly countered that. The Jesus People challenged the 'many paths' relativism of their day, countering those who had been duped into thinking that all religious truth was equally valid. Bible-oriented Christians have always challenged that relativistic idea and will continue to do so.

## Why relativism?

What factors fuel the acceptance of relativism? How is it that our society has become so vulnerable to relativism?

Pride is reason number one. By pride, I mean that we assume that what we believe must be true. Most of us are proud. Even those who might be described as lacking in self-esteem can be proud. In fact, I think that a lack of self-esteem can even exacerbate pride. When a person is confident, the more likely he or she is to be open-minded.

What about you? Do you dig in your heels if challenged about what you believe? Do you feel stepped on, slighted or rejected if someone happens to disagree with you? Are you open to investigating the claims of Christ? Is it possible that he just might be the only way to the one true God?

A second reason for the uncritical acceptance of relativism is that we often lack the boldness to say that something is categorically wrong. There is a certain fear we have — an aversion to being singled out. We are like politicians, in a sense. We know which way the wind is blowing and we are fearful of going against it. We would rather blend in, be accepted, go with the flow and be viewed as intelligent and understanding. We do not want to be classified with religious extremists, narrow-minded bigots, Bible-thumping, wild-eyed fundamentalists, and so on. Open, accepting, broad-minded, educated, sophisticated and mature — these are the labels we crave. Once others see you are going against the stream and making a stand, you will have to pay a price — especially if the stand is that Jesus is the only way to the Father.

A third reason why we tend to accept whatever is popular in our culture is that we often do not exert mental energy to think for ourselves. Lazy minds do not think things through and ask tough questions such as: 'Wait a minute, how could everything be true all at once?' This is not too flattering, I grant you, but thinking can be a laborious and difficult process. After all, if we hear it on television, and the people at school, or at work, or around town are all saying the same thing, it is easier to just go along with it.

A fourth reason we are vulnerable to relativism is that we have uncritically endorsed the concept of diversity. There is much of value in upholding contemporary concepts of diversity. People should not be discriminated against for simply being. Cultural and racial differences contribute to the magnificent kaleidoscope of life — this is the best part of diversity. I may not agree with certain lifestyles and types of behaviour but as long as they are not criminal, I need to uphold common civil rights. Everyone has the right to 'life, liberty and the pursuit of happiness', even if certain non-criminal behaviour clashes with biblical ethics. I am not the judge and jury, but I know that God will be just and I can leave it with him. We take this too far, however, when we are unable to say that something is wrong. Many people have problems with Christians because we stand for truth and can say that certain things are wrong, or even evil. If some religious group attempts to deny the truth of the gospel of Jesus Christ, we cannot say 'Amen' to it. We can say, 'No, that is not true.' And we do. And we must.

Some of the staunchest supporters of relativism are atheists — at least logically, if not actually. If there is no God, there is no absolute truth, only concepts that are of value in the common experience of living. Lawbreakers and anarchists tend towards relativism, generally out of an unconscious fear of a God who would hold them to account. These are practical atheists, if not actual atheists. Sometimes people can reject objective truth, especially the existence of a holy and righteous God, simply because instinctually such a notion seems to inhibit certain freedom and fun — and by this I mean sin.

Maybe it would be helpful, if you are a relativist, to ask yourself *why* you are. Is it because you have no god, or are afraid that if there is a God you are going to be in big trouble? Is it pride? Is it rebellion? Is it because you want to be free to indulge your desires and you cannot stand the idea of a powerful and holy God who will judge you?

## Major world religions

As an illustration of what I have been driving at, I am going to briefly examine some of the world's major religious teachings. Be aware that most of us only get 'Westernized versions' of the world's religions, so some readers may not recognize the views I will be portraying.

In 1967, I was conducting a Bible study in the Krishna Temple in San Francisco. Swami Bhaktivedanta, from India, had a version of Hinduism he called 'Krishna Consciousness'. On the temple's walls were pictures of Jesus. He particularly liked the Roman Catholic version of Christianity with the sentimental renditions of the heart of Jesus and pictures of Mary and various saints; quite a few of these could be found throughout the temple. Swami wanted to show that he was open to all religions. He taught that Jesus was an avatar, a reincarnation of Krishna, and so a special religious figure. 'We adore Jesus and we worship Jesus too,' he told me. But, after his chief devotee was converted to Christ through my witness, the Swami tore down all the religious pictures and ordered me out of the temple — permanently. That was the end of his relativism. The Swami knew that Krishna Consciousness was not compatible with Christianity and it was rather deceitful of him to imply that it was. His actions revealed his true thinking.

Hinduism and some forms of Buddhism are based upon what is called Monism. This means there is no objective reality but only Oneness. The whole point of yoga (which is Hindu) and Zen (which is the Buddhist counterpart) is to discover that there is no reality other than oneness or nothingness. It excludes what is referred to as 'separate reality'. And enlightenment, which is the goal of the religious discipline, is that the devotee spiritually comprehends or merges with nothingness or oneness — and thus becomes detached from suffering and/or escapes the great cycle of reincarnation. Striving for, and maybe achieving, such a 'spiritual' plane can be exhilarating and may severely challenge the body and mind, but the doctrine and spirituality behind these practices do not mesh with Christianity.

Knowledgeable Hindus and Buddhists are aware of the incompatibility between Christianity and their own teachings. For instance, Christian teaching does not demand that the reality of the world be denied. But Eastern religious gurus, spiritual entrepreneurs that they are, sell a version which they calculate will be compatible with Western sensibilities. The result is that many, who uncritically champion diversity and relativism, are fooled. Mature Christians should not be so easily deceived that they would say 'yes' to such a mind-numbing amalgamation.

Hinduism and Buddhism are not related to, or connected with, the Bible. However Islam, which was developed in the sixth and seventh centuries, is tied to the Bible. Islam is not based on Monism but does have some similarities to Judaism and Christianity — however, it is vastly different from Christianity. Compare the concepts of God in Islam and Christianity and make up your own mind.

What did Mohammed teach? He taught that the Bible was a sacred writing and to respect Jesus was fine. But, Mohammed taught that he himself, and the revelation supposedly given to him, superseded all that went before. The result is that Christians are considered infidels and Jesus is no longer the unique and eternal Son of the Father, crucified, resurrected, Lord and Saviour, the way, the truth and the life, but something else. For the Muslim, Jesus becomes a strange religious figure and not at all what the Scriptures reveal. Do I have to embrace the Muslim view of Jesus? No! Can I disagree and risk seeming to reject diversity and relativism? Yes, I can.

Before Christianity, there was Judaism. Christianity is not independent of Judaism, but comes naturally out of it. If the Jewish religious leaders of Jesus' day had embraced him as the prophesied Messiah, there would have been no Christianity — only fulfilled Judaism. The early Christians were all Jews; some of the Jewish leaders and priests became believers in Jesus as Messiah. Official Judaism resisted Jesus and continues to resist to this day.

Despite the status of Judaism as a major world religion, I do not accept its rejection of who Jesus was and is. Relativism would have me minimize this conflict, if not ignore it altogether. Certainly it is politically correct to be inclusive, but that is simply a wrong-headed adherence to postmodern concepts of diversity.

## A new medium

Have you seen the television programme hosted by Robert Stack called *Unsolved Mysteries*? I saw an episode which focused on a psychic. Police authorities had brought him in as a consultant on unsolved criminal investigations. He received messages and recorded the message on a pad of paper. This is frequently called automatic writing — where some spiritual entity takes control of a person and downloads messages.

Psychics sometimes appear to get it right and they do have a source of knowledge. In one segment of the show, someone who had lost a close relative was in tremendous grief. The psychic was brought in for consultation. He recounted some things that only a relative would know and convinced the grieving and, I might add, vulnerable person, that he could be trusted. The psychic said, 'I have a message for you that your relative is doing fine and so don't feel guilty.' It was the same tiresome story, 'They are okay; you are okay, and everything is fine.'

The psychic was believable because *he actually was* in contact with spiritual beings that, in a way we do not comprehend, had access to supernatural knowledge. He himself did not realize that he had been deceived by these beings.

Someone might object: 'The psychic was a considerate, pleasant and caring person.' The apostle Paul, who understood mediums, said, 'No wonder, for even Satan disguises himself as an angel of light. So it is not strange if his servants also disguise themselves as servants of right-eousness' (2 Cor. 11:14–15). I am not contending that the psychic was necessarily deliberately being deceptive. He believed that what he was doing was valid; he believed his 'gifts' were good not evil. He, like other mediums and psychics, was sincere and he was accurate about some things. But he was deceived about the source of his knowledge and he was deceiving others.

## What is truth?

Jesus and Pontius Pilate, the Roman governor of Judea, once discussed the nature of truth. Their conversation is recorded in John 18:33–38:

> Pilate entered the praetorium again and called Jesus, and said to him, 'Are you the King of the Jews?' Jesus answered, 'Do you say this of your own accord, or did others say it to you about me?' Pilate answered, 'Am I a Jew? Your own nation and the chief priests have handed you over to me; what have you done?' Jesus answered, 'My kingship is not of this world; if my kingship were of this world, my servants would fight, that I might not be handed over to the Jews; but my kingship is not from the world.' Pilate said to him, 'So you are a king?' Jesus answered, 'You say that I am a king. For this I was born, and for this I have come into the world, to bear witness to the truth. Every one who is of the truth hears my voice.' Pilot said to him, 'What is truth?'

Pilate was right. The great issue is 'What is truth?'

As humbling as it might be, we must admit that we do not have the truth and what we say or believe is not always true. Jesus himself is truth. One day everyone will know this. Everyone who has embraced error, everyone who has been duped, tricked and deceived, will one day understand without question that Jesus is truth. This knowledge comes either at death, or, should we be alive when Jesus returns, at the Second Advent or coming of Jesus. These events will either thrill us or devastate us. Either they will be the fulfilment of that which the believer has longed for, or they will be the cause of ultimate panic for the unbeliever. In Philippians 2:10 Paul said, 'At the name of Jesus every knee should bow, in heaven and on earth and under the earth.' We will all bow the knee, but for those who have been deceived it will be too late.

## Hard to hear

From time to time Jesus told those who followed him some rather shocking things. For example in John 6:65, he said to a large group of followers: 'This is why I told you that no one can come to me unless it is granted him by the Father.' The fairly large group of disciples, far more than just the twelve apostles, might have understood him to say something like:

'Become a disciple of Hillel, or a disciple of Shammai, (two of the leading Rabbinical schools of the first century), or follow one of the many messianic pretenders who rise up periodically and announce they will free Israel from Roman rule. You can follow them. If a Greek philosopher should happen to travel to Israel, you might follow him, but you cannot come to me unless it is granted to you by the Father.'

Now consider the reaction: 'After this many of his disciples drew back and no longer went about with him' (John 6:66). They reasoned, 'We have heard enough. We are not going to buy into this narrow concept.' And they left.

Jesus said to the twelve, 'Do you also wish to go away?' (John 6:67) Peter answered him, 'Lord, to whom shall we go? You have the words of eternal life; and we have believed, and have come to know, that you are the Holy One of God.'

Jesus was uncompromising. He knew there were some who would go away. But those whom he had called — the twelve, the chosen — he knew they would not go away. They were going to stick with him; he was the Holy One of God. He could say with all authority, 'I am the way, and the truth, and the life. No one comes to the Father but by me.'

# CHAPTER 6

# You have been duped if you think you are good enough

L et us now consider the tremendous effort we make to avoid the truth about ourselves. We know that generally with maturity comes the recognition that we are not perfect. However, there is a certain lack of humility that leads each of us to believe that the path we are on is the right one. Once again, human pride raises its head.

## A personal testimony

I remember how frustrated I was with certain Christians who challenged my belief system, confused and ill-formed as it was.

I was twenty-one years old when I first began to be confronted with Christianity. I was a medic in the U.S. Air Force by night and a college student by day. My estimation of myself was quite high and I thought, 'How dare these people tell me what is right and wrong?' The truth is that I was headed down the wrong road! My sense of who I was and what I was doing seemed fine to me and I did not have the strength, personal security or self-esteem to be able to say, 'Maybe I do not know the truth. Maybe I should reconsider what it is I really do believe.' Besides, I judged them to be less bright and educated than myself.

## Jesus confronted error

Once again I am reminded of how Jesus confronted the wrong-headed notions of people in his day. We find a number of examples of this in Matthew 23. Jesus said, 'Woe to you, scribes and Pharisees, hypocrites!

for you cleanse the outside of the cup and of the plate, but inside they are full of extortion and rapacity' (Matt. 23:25). This indictment requires some explanation. Jesus was referring to kosher food laws: the preparation of the Sabbath meal, the ritual washing of the vessels, cups and pots used in cooking and the careful preparation of food itself. These dietary and ritual laws had to be observed by orthodox Jews. The scribes and the Pharisees were careful in their observance and taught others to do the same. Jesus meant that although the religious teachers *outwardly* observed the myriad of kosher food regulations, they were corrupt inwardly. 'Extortion and rapacity' were the words Jesus used. He meant that they cheated the common person and were self-indulgent or intemperate themselves. They were careful to clean the outside of the utensils and dishes while at the same time making sure they filled their pockets with money and their cups with wine. That which had the appearance of stringent observance was simply greed and gluttony.

Then he said, 'You blind Pharisee! first cleanse the inside of the cup and of the plate, that the outside also may be clean' (Matt. 23:26). There is a great deal that could be said about that passage, but the point I want to make is that Jesus had the strength and courage to be confrontational to these spiritually complacent people.

Jesus was just a young man when he said these things. He had no formal education behind him nor political or religious standing or authority. He had no major following. He had a few disciples, but they were all from Galilee, and that was not considered a commendation. His followers did not include anyone of note and Jesus was speaking to people who were probably twice his age — mature men who were esteemed in the community.

He said, 'Woe to you.' He called them hypocrites. He said they were blind. How strong Jesus was! But why would he take such a risk?

If Jesus had been a student at a typical seminary, he would probably have been expelled. He might have been told, 'That is not the way to relate to people. You have no right to be so harsh and judgemental.' Jesus, however, was about something more important than seeking approval. He had in mind that the Father who had sent him loved these people who were righteous in their own eyes. Jesus attempted to show them that, despite their religious good deeds, they were not good enough for God.

## The text: Romans 3:9–18

In Romans 3:9, Paul states: 'What then: Are we Jews any better off? No, not at all; for I have already charged that all men, both Jews and Greeks, are under the power of sin.' Paul declares that every person, regardless of race or religion, is under the power of sin. 'Under the power of sin' means that not only are we sinful, but that we are also under the control of sin. The apostle then strings together a number of quotes, mainly from the Psalms, but also from Isaiah, to prove his point:

> 'None is righteous, no, not one; no one understands, no one seeks
>    for God. All have turned aside, together they have gone wrong;
>    no one does good, not even one.'
> 'Their throat is an open grave, they use their tongues to deceive.'
> 'The venom of asps is under their lips.'
> 'Their mouth is full of curses and bitterness.'
> 'Their feet are swift to shed blood, in their paths are ruin and misery,
>    and the way of peace they do not know.'
> 'There is no fear of God before their eyes' (Rom. 3:10b–18).

The words 'turned aside' are essentially the fundamental definition of sin. Only a few times in my ministry have I encountered someone who is convinced that he or she is not sinful. And of these, most were locked up in San Quentin Prison and insisted that they had been manipulated and victimized by society and were therefore not blameworthy in any way. But, this extreme aside, most will grant that they are not perfect, or even close to it.

## An objection

Some might object: 'I don't agree with that analysis. I am not like that at all.' Would there be such a person? There are such, as I mentioned. I was one myself, an expert at denial. I had no understanding of the holiness of God and had, unsurprisingly, developed a standard *I* was comfortable with. There was always someone worse than myself — someone from an article in the newspaper, or a character in a history book. Abnormal psychology, being one of my favourite subjects, acquainted me with people who were indeed worse than me — or so I thought. My criterion was sufficiently low so that I looked good *in comparison*. It was simply a matter of finding the right standard to compare myself with.

But the Scripture states that there is not *even one* person who is good enough for God. And here is the real trouble: we simply do not understand the holiness or purity of God. We do not understand that the Creator God dwells in unapproachable light; we do not realize that no sin can come before him, absolutely none!

Consider the two great commandments. First, 'You shall love the Lord your God with all your heart and with all your soul and with all your mind and will all your strength.' And second, 'You shall love your neighbor as yourself' (Mark 12:30–31). Can *anyone* claim to have kept these commandments perfectly *every* moment of every day, year after year? Certainly not! How about loving our neighbour? Does anyone want to claim this? Most of us have a hard time loving ourselves. This is the initial problem, but it is still a breaking of the commandment, because we are created in God's image. We are actually commanded to love ourselves.

These commandments are the highest of standards and we do not, and cannot, measure up. I cannot say that for even one minute I have kept these commandments. Try as I might, I cannot obey them. These highest expressions of the law of God reveal the fact that I am a lawbreaker. Indeed, there is none good, not even one (Rom. 3:12). We have broken God's law; we are not good enough.

Someone might reason: 'Well, that is what the Bible says, but I do not care about the rules and commandments in the Bible.' And, indeed, maybe there is no known standard in the world that matters to such a person. Convenient and self-serving as this position might be, the problem remains that there is a righteous and holy God who holds us accountable. It is easy to see why atheism is such a draw — get rid of the authority and the big accountant in the sky, and then we do not have to worry about not being good enough. And for those who are able to swallow such a lie, go your way, but it is the way that leads to death (Prov. 14:12).

Reading Romans 3 makes one think that Paul had been reading our own newspapers or watching our evening news broadcasts. Life was just the same as it is right now. I do not think the human race gets worse as the generations go by. Some people say, 'This generation is worse than any previous generation.' I do not agree. I think evil, and the human condition, have been constant from the earliest days to our own. Perhaps we are now more keenly aware of evil because of the media's instantaneous and widespread reach. One day things will worsen, as Paul explains in 2 Timothy 3:1–5:

> But understand this, that in the last days there will come times of stress. For men will be lovers of self, lovers of money, proud, arrogant,

abusive, disobedient to their parents, ungrateful, unholy, inhuman, implacable, slanderers, profligates, fierce, haters of good, treacherous, reckless, swollen with conceit, lovers of pleasure rather than lovers of God, holding the form of religion but denying the power of it. Avoid such people.

Are we improving? Are we becoming better people? Are we evolving to a higher plane of consciousness? I do not think we are. I agree with one of the great Old Testament prophets, Jeremiah, who said, 'Can a leopard change his spots?' (Jer. 13:23, paraphrase) A leopard cannot do so and neither can we. We can change in minor ways, adjust to our environments and life circumstances, but we are who we are. The truth is, we are dead in our trespasses and sins (Eph. 2:1). We are lost, we are blind, we are deaf, and even the message of the love of God seems foolish to us (1 Cor. 1:18).

## The image of God

The human condition is magnified because of who we are. We are made in the image of God, and wonderfully made at that. We are the pinnacle of creation, of even greater stature than the angels of heaven, who are not made in God's image. And, for that reason, the Creator loves us. Each person is a special, unique creation. We are capable of thinking grand thoughts, performing loving acts and creating wondrous works of art and music. We are capable of heroic, selfless exploits; we are able to endure the worst conditions and still retain our humanity.

Our fall into sin, then, is truly tragic and our restoration to full humanity — our rescue from the abyss of hell — is truly amazing. But, and let me emphasize this as best I can, *we must realize that we are lost and in a desperate situation before we can be found*. We must see we have bought into a lie before we can see the truth.

## A test: Just how duped are you?

Below is a test I have devised that may reveal just how deceived you might be. I developed it on the basis of my own experience as a duped person and my intimate relationship with deceived people.

*1. Do you think you can bargain with and influence God?*
*Can you perform a good work that will be enough to earn God's forgive-ness? Does it seem reasonable that if you gave up some sin and started*

*going to church and praying and giving money to charity, then this would*
*be enough to earn God's favour?*

How unjust it would be if some privileged people were able to manipulate
God! We are all powerless to do so. We have no bargaining power at all
and no possible way of influencing God. What could we do that would
appease a holy God? In comparison with our sins and offences against
him, our 'righteous' acts could never measure up or influence him. We
must recognize that we are finite creatures who have rebelled against the
infinite Creator.

*2. Do you believe in a 'heavenly scale of justice'?*
*Some imagine that God has a set of scales, one in either hand, and that*
*he weighs our good and bad deeds. The prospect is that our good deeds*
*weigh more than our bad deeds — meaning we will go to heaven. This is*
*a slight variation from the idea that we are good enough.*

This is wishful thinking at best. This concept is without any biblical warrant
and ignores the nature and power of sin. Sin impugns God's holiness.
One sin is enough to tip the scale completely — no so-called balance can
be achieved.

Imagine, for a moment, a system whereby your good and bad deeds are
weighed against each other. How is it that you would even know your status
with God? Would you know when your good deeds were more than your
bad? This assumes that you had the capacity to know what constituted a
good or bad deed. The whole thing is absurd. I would hate to have anything to do with a God who judged me on my deeds, good or bad. It would
produce anxiety and hold me in emotional and spiritual dread.

*3. Do you think you are God?*
*Some imagine, 'I don't have to worry about sin because I am god myself.'*

Adam and Eve were told by the serpent that once the forbidden fruit was
eaten they would be like God (Gen. 3:5). They did eat and the result was
that their innocence and freedom ended and they were excluded from
paradise and God's presence. We are not God, we are not part of God, we
will not become God — we will always be who we are right now. Therefore,
our sin is a real problem. It will not go away, unless it is cleansed and
washed away through trusting in Jesus.

Yet people will believe they are gods. After all, if you are god then of
course you do not need forgiveness.

*4. Do you believe in a god that is immoral or has no morality at all?*
*The Graeco-Roman gods were worshipped for a millennium and a half.*
*Contemporary versions of the ancient deities are worshipped by some*
*today — albeit in different guises. One of the reasons they were popular*
*is because they had no moral ethic. The gods themselves were immoral,*
*changing and sometimes capricious and vain. Yet people loved these*
*gods. Much of that religion had to do with charms, superstition and good*
*and bad fortune. The gods were fantastic and fanciful — comparable to*
*soap opera, film, sport and rock stars today.*

We create gods and goddesses, as the Greeks and Romans did, and we
feel comfortable with those who will excuse our sin and not call us to
account. These flawed gods of our making will not expect holiness and
personal integrity, though they may reward submission and worship.
These gods come in many sizes and shapes, and will vary from culture to
culture. They may not be labelled gods at all, but will be treated as such.
We know these are our gods because we look to them for comfort and
encouragement when things are not going our way and when we do not
want to turn from our sinful ways.

What has the test revealed? How did you score? Have you fallen into
any of these deceptions? Your responses are very revealing about the state
of your heart right now.

## Addiction

Essentially this chapter has consisted of a description of methods we employ
in order to avoid the biblical truth that we have broken God's commandments and are, in fact, slaves of sin. In the 12-step programmes (such as
Alcoholics Anonymous), it is called addiction — we are addicted to sinful ways.

In a surprisingly personal manner, Paul described this power of sin in a
letter to the church at Rome. From this letter we can see that Paul knew
his own sinfulness.

> But I am carnal, sold under sin. I do not understand my own
> actions. For I do not do what I want, but I do the very thing I hate.
> Now if I do what I do not want, I agree that the law is good. So
> then it is no longer I that do it, but sin which dwells within me.
> For I know that nothing good dwells within me, that is, in my
> flesh. I can will what is right, but I cannot do it. For I do not do
> the good I want, but the evil I do not want is what I do. Now if I

do what I do not want, it is no longer I that do it, but sin which dwells within me.

So I find it to be a law that when I want to do right, evil lies close at hand. For I delight in the law of God, in my inmost self, but I see in my members another law at war with the law of my mind and making me captive to the law of sin which dwells in my members. Wretched man that I am! Who will deliver me from this body of death? (Rom. 7:14–24).

This is what Paul says of himself. Sin is within him, and it is powerful, baffling, mysterious and addictive — this is the nature of sin.

Paul is not absolving himself of responsibility for his sin, but he was a man who was willing to admit the truth about himself. 'For I know that nothing good dwells within me, that is, in my flesh. I can will what is right, but I cannot do it.' Paul is speaking of himself in the present tense; he is not referring to some point before his conversion to Christ. As a Christian — a called, chosen apostle of Jesus — he says such things about himself. What was true of Paul is true of you and me as well: 'For I do not do the good I want, but the evil I do not want is what I do.'

This sounds hopeless and as if we might just as well give up. Paul has not finished, however, and he cries out, 'Wretched man that I am! Who will deliver me from this body of death?' His answer follows: 'Thanks be to God through Jesus Christ our Lord! ... For the law of the Spirit of life in Christ Jesus has set me free from the law of sin and death' (Rom. 7:25; 8:2).

## The difference

What is the difference between 'Paul the Christian' and 'Paul the non-Christian'? Prior to Paul's conversion he was hopeless and did not have the power of Jesus in his life (Eph. 1:19–20). That is the difference. And we are the same — we are without ability either to cease from sin or to forgive ourselves. We have no ability. We are trapped by our own lust, anger and greed.

We cannot solve the problem of sin in our lives. But Jesus can, because he took our sin upon himself on the cross — the cross is the victory! Forgiveness is not *achieved*, but rather *received*. The Christian has received the righteousness of God through Jesus Christ. This righteousness is placed upon the believer. Or to put it another way, we have put on Christ. In Christ, believers have victory over sin; it no longer overwhelms us. Forgiven and indwelt by the Holy Spirit, we may have struggles, but the power of Jesus over sin is now ours.

We must realize that Christians fight battles and wage war against sin, but they no longer fight in their own strength. Paul says, 'Thanks be to God through Jesus Christ our Lord!' This is a concise way of saying that it is now Jesus who is our strength — Jesus is our righteousness.

If we think we are good enough in and of ourselves, we are still deceived. Our only hope and strength can come from Jesus. We need to recognize our powerlessness and fall on our knees before God and seek him — that is where, and through whom, the victory over sin is won.

I am not good enough. I do not want even to imagine that I am good enough. If it all depended on me, it would be a hopeless situation. Of course, most religions preach a 'Be good, do good,' message. I would rather be an ethical atheist or agnostic than be involved in a religion that kept telling me I was only as good as my last good deed. How often religions manipulate us through guilt!

Genuine Christianity points to Jesus, who completely forgives and saves apart from anything we can do. If I look to myself, I am lost and in despair and will never come to any kind of assurance and security. There is only one who was good enough and that is Jesus. I look to Jesus. He is my righteousness; in him is power over sin. There is no other answer. There is no trick or five quick, easy rules. We cannot take a workshop, or seminar, or apply good principles. There is only one thing we can do — look to Jesus! He is the Saviour. He is the righteous one who was able to pay the price of our sins and free us from the power of sin in our lives. He is the righteous, Holy One of God. Assurance and security are to be found in Jesus and Jesus himself. Look to Jesus and be saved.

# CHAPTER 7

# You have been duped if you think you can ignore your conscience, the Bible or the church

T oday, many people know little of the Bible or Christianity. A high percentage of the present generation (those in their twenties and thirties) has neither been to a church nor read a page of the Bible. My own generation generally knows something of the Bible and Christianity because many have attended church services or Sunday school at some point in their lives. Men and women born after 1965 often know little of the Bible or Christianity except what has filtered down to them through the media or school textbooks — information which may not be entirely accurate. And their children have landed right in the midst of a post-Christian culture. I know that the youth around my home in Marin County, Northern California, know more of yoga and Zen Buddhism than they do of biblical Christianity. My intent is to communicate with and present Jesus to those who have little grasp of the gospel message.

I am struck by how many people simply go about their lives ignoring and dismissing the Bible and the church, and to a lesser extent, their conscience — without cause. If you are among those who know little of Christianity, please carefully consider this chapter for it may have more relevance for your life than is first apparent.

## Jesus confronted deceived people

In Jesus' day, there were many who ignored or dismissed the Jewish Bible (the Old Testament), the religious establishment and their God-given conscience. Jesus especially confronted those who had rejected, twisted or misunderstood the Hebrew Scriptures. In addition, he spoke harsh words to those religious types who looked clean outwardly but inwardly were not. Here we find Jesus using the 'woe' word again: 'Woe to you, scribes and Pharisees, hypocrites! for you are like whitewashed tombs, which outwardly appear beautiful, but within they are full of dead men's bones and all uncleanness. So you also outwardly appear righteous to men, but within you are full of hypocrisy and iniquity' (Matt. 23:27–28).

These religious leaders, for the most part, refused to consider the arguments Jesus presented. They ignored their sacred Scriptures as well as their own consciences. But before we think too much of ourselves, we must admit that they are not very different from the self-deluded of every generation. In fact, it is not difficult for me to identify with them myself. Except for God's grace, I am just like them.

## The text: Hebrews 3:7–11

Therefore, as the Holy Spirit says,
'Today, when you hear his voice,
>    do not harden your hearts as in the rebellion,
>    on the day of testing in the wilderness,
>    where your fathers put me to the test
>    and saw my works for forty years.
Therefore I was provoked with that generation,
>    and said, "They always go astray in their hearts;
>    they have not known my ways."
As I swore in my wrath,
"They shall never enter my rest"' (Heb. 3:7–11).

The writer of Hebrews is quoting Psalm 95:7–8 where the psalmist is referring to the Exodus of the nation of Israel from Egypt, under the leadership of Moses. They ended up wandering around the Arabian wilderness for forty years because of their disobedience. Eventually they ran out of water and then complained, 'Moses, what did you do? You brought us into the desert so we can die of thirst! We could have died in Egypt' (Exod. 17:3, paraphrase).

## The witness of the conscience

The psalmist testified that the wandering Israelites had hardened their hearts not only against Moses, but against God too. Is this our condition? We also go astray in our hearts.

'Heart' means the core of us, our inner being, and includes our conscience — that inner sense of right and wrong. A stony or cold heart makes us vulnerable to being tricked and deceived. Our conscience does not work well when we go against it over and over again— it becomes dull and insensitive. It is then that we are especially vulnerable to deception.

While we are growing up, things can happen to us that cause bitterness or anger to take root and, as a result, we become hardened inside. Anger towards a father, a mother or another authority figure may develop and somehow we become callous towards God, the Bible or the church. Maybe the psychological process of transference explains it; the anger that builds up inside us is transferred to something other than the real source. Or, things happen to us as adults and we become discouraged, frustrated, even terribly hurt, and our insides turn to stone as a defence — the result is that our conscience, our heart, is damaged. I have seen this time and again in over three decades of pastoral ministry and twenty-one years of volunteer work at San Quentin Prison. There are many, many people with cold and bruised hearts.

We are 'blamers'. We tend to look for reasons why something happened and fix blame on someone. We are comforted, perhaps in a false way, when we can blame someone or something outside ourselves when things go wrong. We do not want to feel that we might be a part of the problem. I remember how quick I was to blame God for tragedies and, of course, also to blame the church, the Bible or Christians. It was an unconscious process but powerful all the same. The result was that I was able to reject and ignore the spiritual influences around me.

The last verse, Hebrews 3:11, deserves some consideration: 'As I swore in my wrath, "They shall never enter my rest."' 'Wait a minute,' someone might object; 'I thought this was a loving God here! What is this, "swearing in his wrath"? And look at the terrible penalty, "They shall never enter my rest."'

If I did not understand the God of the Bible, I would be offended by Hebrews 3:11. Some have wanted to draw a distinction between the 'wrathful' God of the Old Testament and the 'loving' God of the New Testament. Christians, however, and the Bible itself, testify that he is one and the same God all the way through Scripture. There are different emphases through the various books of the Bible but the key that we need to remember is the holiness of God — perhaps his chief attribute. Holiness means a setting apart and separateness from all that is morally or ethically impure. If God is actually holy, then he must by his very nature hate and judge sin. God is not filled with an anger that is characterized by jumping up and down in a rage, like people do. Rather his anger is a righteous anger against the sin and impurity that offend his very character.

The expression, 'As I swore in my wrath,' is anthropomorphic — attributing human emotions to God. This is a literary device commonly used in the Bible to enable men and women to understand aspects of God's character. When it is all broken down and considered, God would not be truly God if he were not righteous and just and thus full of wrath against sin.

What if nothing mattered to God? What if he did not care? What if God himself was sinful? Would this God deserve our praise and worship? What would it mean for people to be like this God? It is important to see who God really is or we may be tempted to close our minds to him. So it is not surprising to find that God would be offended and angry at sin.

## Miraculous interventions — how we ignore them

People commonly report miraculous experiences. Some such events happened to me when I was growing up. A few times I have thought to myself, 'Philpott, you ought to be dead. How is it that you are still living? How did you survive that?'

One narrow escape occurred when I was riding in my friend Bill's first car, a 1956 Chevy. We were barely sixteen years old and Bill had recently learned how to drive. Attempting to cross an intersection, Bill did not see another car speeding down the hill. It hit the side of our Chevy and sent the vehicle right through a stone wall. Bill and I have visited that site more than once and wondered how it was that we escaped with our lives. We were bloodied but we survived. Was that a miraculous intervention?

Usually, immediately following a miraculous intervention we have a brief window of time when we think to ourselves, 'There is a God. I ought to pay attention.' Or, it might be that a close friend, a brother or sister, is tragically hurt or even killed. There is the window again, but it is not long before it is closed and our hearts return to their usual cold and numb state.

## The apostle Paul and the conscience

Paul, in his letter to the church in Rome, deals with the conscience. Some of this may be difficult to understand, but I will explain the essentials below. Paul writes, 'When Gentiles who have not the law do by nature what the law requires, they are a law to themselves, even though they do not have the law. They show that what the law requires is written on their hearts, while their conscience also bears witness and their conflicting thoughts accuse or perhaps excuse them' (Rom. 2:14–15).

The Jewish nation had been given God's commandments through Moses. However, Gentiles (non-Jews) had not been given the law of God in this way. The point is that even though the Gentiles were not directly warned about murder, adultery, stealing, lying, and so on, they none the less viewed them as wrong anyway. Paul argues that this illustrates that there is a conscience in each of us, regardless of our background.

I am not aware of any cultures that do not have prohibitions against murder. There may be cultures that condone incest, adultery, lying and stealing, but I think it is safe to say that, in general, whether a culture has been exposed to the law of Moses or not, there are going to be certain basic restrictions and prohibitions. Paul taught that this is evidence of a conscience, a sense of right and wrong that is hard-wired into us by the Creator. Paul argues that Gentiles who do not have the law of Moses are also guilty before God because they have a conscience and know, inwardly, what is right and wrong.

When our conscience is ignored or repeatedly violated, it becomes ineffective. To constantly ignore our conscience is to open our minds up to being deceived, and this is very dangerous. A sociopath or psychopath is a person with an abnormal psychological condition in which the conscience has failed almost completely. Such a condition often leads to a life in prison. It leads to eternal death as well.

## The witness of the Bible

Secondly, we have the witness of the Bible. I will deal more extensively with the Bible later in the book but for now I will simply hit the highlights.

The current generation has little knowledge of the Bible, or so the polls tell us. But, it is interesting how the words of Scripture get out a little bit at a time and I, like Paul, am happy that the gospel is disseminated by whatever means (Phil. 2:13–15).

Sometimes you find parts of the gospel in cartoons. The late Charles Schulz would slip it in every once in a while in a *Peanuts* strip. Charles Schulz was a Christian. Johnny Hart, the author of the comic strip *B.C.*, received some bad press with a piece in which one of his caveman characters asked, 'What do dead atheists, agnostics and saints have in common?' The answer in the next frame was: 'They all know there is a God.' The cartoonist attracted a lot of criticism for it — he was not politically correct, I suppose. Yet, there was some of the gospel and some truth that was published.

In my favorite movie, *High Noon*, there is some gospel too. In this old black-and-white film with Gary Cooper and Grace Kelly, there is a scene that takes place in a church. A hymn is being sung — and there the gospel is heard in the words of the hymn. How about Robert Duvall's movie, *The Apostle*? A lot of gospel found its way into that production.

And I thank God for Larry King and his *Larry King Live* CNN programme. I do not know of anything on television, short of the religious channels, that has more gospel in it than Larry King does — and it is not his intention to proclaim the gospel at all. He brings people on the programme who are not afraid to talk about Jesus. He interviews people who do not cave in to the standard ideas on ecumenicity. King often has Billy Graham or Franklin Graham, but my favourite is Billy Graham's daughter, Anne Graham Lotz. The Grahams are not light on religion!

Despite the bias against the Christian message, it still finds its way even into non-religious, mainstream media formats. Remember the song John Denver sang about late-night radio? One line in the song says, 'The Lord is still my shepherd, but those preachers gotta go. Best friend when I'm lonely is the late night radio.' If you happen to be driving across the country, sometimes about all you can pick up on your car radio will be a preacher. Somehow the message is heard.

The tragedy in America on 11 September 2001 provides an example of what I mean. Youth With A Mission (YWAM) had dozens of young people praying for those at Ground Zero. Their mission effort even got some good publicity. I rejoiced to hear about the Southern Baptists' determination to bring a gospel witness to the 2002 Winter Olympics in Salt Lake City, Utah. The coverage they received was mostly negative, of course, but the message of Jesus and the cross was heard.

Consider the Gideon Bibles in motel and hotel rooms, or the thousands of missionary groups around the world, some of which even send missionaries to America. People preach on street corners — often not well I grant you — but they are getting the message out. It troubles me when the gospel is communicated poorly, but the message is still being heard. For every listener, there is a preacher. And there is still the old-fashioned way — the personal testimony — and this goes on constantly throughout the world. As we say, 'One beggar telling another beggar where to find bread.'

The witness of the Bible and its gospel continues to be heard in snippets here and there, even through overheard conversations. People have even overheard the gospel in restaurants, perhaps being discussed by a party at a nearby table.

'Bible'. There is an impact when the word is simply mentioned. Or, what about the sight of a Bible? The focus goes immediately to it. And inside, its words can be sharp, different, strong and convicting as the Holy Spirit empowers it. There is nothing magical about the book itself. But it is the inspired Word of God and the Holy Spirit uses it in amazing ways.

The Bible is not like any other so-called sacred scripture. I have read them — the Qur'an, the Book of Mormon, the Urantia Book, and the Course in Miracles books — and how different the Bible is! No matter how wonderfully constructed and sublime, great prose and poetry still lack the substance of the Scriptures.

Ignoring the Bible is a mistake and will eventually lead to solid self-deception. It is only through the Scriptures that we know what is spiritually true. Without the Bible as a benchmark, we easily fall into error. By it, we evaluate the religious and spiritual claims of impostors. Without the Bible, we have no sure means of drawing lines.

## The witness of the church

Each week thousands of people drive down the street where our Miller Avenue church is located. They may even spot the cross on our roof — a visual testimony to the cross of Jesus Christ. There are also the testimonies of other nearby churches. For example, our good friends at Peace Lutheran Church play the Westminster Chimes on Sunday mornings — a little reminder that the church of Jesus Christ is still here. Yes, the American church has greatly declined, especially here in Northern California, but there are yet hundreds of churches in the Bay area. There are over 100 churches of my own denomination in our region. Some churches are no longer proclaiming the gospel, but many are. You would have to live in a cave in New Mexico or Arizona to avoid the witness of the church altogether. (I doubt whether even hiding in a cave in the desert would prevent some 'ex-Jesus freak' from showing up toting a New Testament!)

Our long Christian history has been marred and scandalized in many ways, but it has been within the church that great awakenings and great revivals have come. Some of these events have radically transformed societies.

Whenever there is a powerful move of the Spirit of God, often the forum and the initial venue has been a local church. We have been commanded by Jesus to preach the gospel to the entire world. The church, the body of Christ, has done that. The witness of the church goes out today.

Even in countries where it is a capital offence to preach Jesus Christ, it is still done. There is not a country in the world where there is not some Christian witness. There has also never been a time when the church has experienced so much persecution — dedicated and systematic persecution. The terrible Roman persecutions of the second, third and fourth centuries are rivalled in ferocity by the persecution experienced today. Yet more people are becoming Christians right now than ever before.

Those who have written the church off, or who ignore it, are in the process of duping themselves. It is out of the church, weak and vulnerable though it may appear, that the gospel goes forth. Nothing will prevail against it. The church belongs to Jesus Christ and it will endure and triumph.

## Three consequences

The first consequence of rejecting the witness of your conscience, the Bible and the church is that you end up fighting against yourself — you become your own worst enemy. This rejection produces an inner stress and tension because it is a denial of how God made us. We were made *for* God. We were made in his image. We were made to know him, and when we reject him and his witnesses, can it produce any good thing?

People are searching for peace. We have anxiety, turmoil and chaos in our minds and hearts. At the very centre of our being, we are tense. I think that some of that must come from the rejection of the witness to the truth that God has provided.

The second consequence of rejecting the witnesses God has given is that the older you get, the more tenaciously you cling to the lies you have embraced. In other words, the older you get, the more rigid and hard your heart tends to become. Having been duped and deceived for so long, you become inflexible and your soul becomes like flint.

It is a special miracle of God when an older person is converted. Most people over fifty are so firmly entrenched in their views that they turn a deaf ear to the message of Jesus. Some, however, are converted and it has happened to a number of people at our church on Miller Avenue.

The third consequence of ignoring your conscience, the Bible and the church is that you are poisoning yourself little by little. It is like the frog in the pot as the water is gradually being heated. Because it happens so gradually, he does not realize that the water is approaching the boiling state.

This is the ultimate spiritual suicide — cutting yourself off from eternal life. Those who reject the gospel have only themselves to blame because the witness of God goes out. You are reading this book — so now you have the testimony of the gospel. Think of all the times you have had something about Jesus or the Bible cross your mind. The truth has come before you; therefore, there is no one to blame but yourself. It has happened little by little, but it is not too late.

I am reminded of the story Jesus told of the rich man and Lazarus, recorded in Luke 16. A rich man accumulated wealth, while a beggar, Lazarus, a righteous person, begged at the rich man's front gate. Lazarus died and went to paradise, or Abraham's bosom. The rich man did not fare so well and went to hell after he died. Yet, the rich man lived in a Jewish community and would have had the witness of the synagogue and Scripture from his youth onwards. He had a conscience, which he ignored; after all, he never bothered to alleviate the suffering of Lazarus. He had evidence of his error from three sources, his conscience, the Scripture and his own religious upbringing, but he ignored and denied them all. The result was not as he hoped, but as he feared — an eternity in hell.

## We don't know what we are doing

Who can insist that they never ignored their conscience, the Bible or the church? I cannot. Does it never occur to us that we are fighting against ourselves? Mostly, we are trying to survive in a confusing, and often brutal, world. I never perceived myself as an evil person who was bent on rebellion against God. That is how it is with most of us — we do not know what we are doing.

Jesus prayed for people like us. He said, 'Father forgive them, they do not know what they do' (Luke 23:34). Right there, he prayed for me and he prayed for you. As a Christian, especially as a gospel preacher, I have a soft heart towards those who are slowly poisoning themselves by rejecting and ignoring the witnesses to the truth of the gospel. Except for a direct intervention by God's Holy Spirit, I would still be in a terrible situation. And the same is true for you.

## A final appeal

Lastly, are you sure, you who have rejected the inner witness, your conscience, the Scripture and the church, that you are right? I know that sometimes it is no more than a knee-jerk reaction. Sometimes it is self-protective; you want to conceal your sin. You may think, 'I am young. I have to be free to be me. I can't be restrained by all of this.' Or perhaps it is a matter of pride and you think, 'I'm right. Don't tell me, I won't listen to you. I am right. How dare you attack what I believe!' Sometimes it is nothing more than conforming to an ungodly world. The world rushes on and it is difficult to swim against the current. It may be the easy way to stand with the secular majority — this is what most people do. They go with the flow and ignore these gospel witnesses.

If the witness of the Bible, the church and your own conscience is nothing and does not bring truth and peace, well then, go your way. Carry on with the way you want. You will go into a godless eternity knowing what you have rejected.

But, I challenge you — find out for yourself. Read about Jesus. Read what Jesus said. Consider this man's life. Can you find a lie on his lips? Can you find an unloving action? Can you find hypocrisy, deceit or insincerity in the man? You cannot! You will find it in the church. Indeed, the Bible may trouble you. You may be confused by your own conscience, but study Jesus, seek him. Look to Jesus. Open the door. He said, 'I stand at the door and knock; if any one hears my voice and opens the door, I will come in to him' (Rev. 3:20). He will soften your hard heart. All the witnesses are one — all are really Jesus. It has been Jesus all along standing at the door and knocking.

# CHAPTER 8

# You have been duped if you think Jesus is merely another spiritual master

W hy would anyone think this anyway? The answer is simple — it is a common understanding of Jesus today, a postmodern cultural myth. I would not hesitate to assert that most people in the world today view Jesus as just one spiritual master among many. Hindus do this, Buddhists do this and groups like the Church of Religious Science, Science of Mind, Scientology, Bahai and Unity do this. Islam does this, too, essentially. Non-Christian religions, along with sects or cults which have perverted the teaching of the Bible or Christianity to suit their own ends, have a vested interest in obscuring what the Bible teaches about Jesus so that they can win a place for their divergent concepts. It suits them to make Jesus into just another spiritual master.

I reject what these world religions teach about the God of the Bible. I am not going to accept their views in the name of diversity. I am not that ecumenical. I will work with people of varying faiths to help alleviate human suffering and work for justice, but I am not going to change my theology, nor am I going to consider that other theologies are somehow compatible with mine. I am not going to do that. I must be honest about it.

## The making of a new Jesus

Now that the church-growth movement in mainstream Christianity is on the wane, trans-religious groups are embracing the techniques that have been used to make evangelical churches grow. 'Trans-religious' means the amalgamation of many different religious traditions. These groups blend together New Age thought, Hinduism and American Buddhism, among others, hoping to broaden their appeal. The success of these spiritual entrepreneurs shows that the application of sophisticated marketing techniques can result in 'church growth' despite the content or spiritual message. These groups give a totally false picture of the true Jesus; they make him into just another spiritual master.

## A new kind of 'church' is coming soon

Gene Edward Veith reported on one such 'church' in the 15 December 2001 edition of *World* magazine. The pastor described his church's philosophy as 'new thought' combined with ancient wisdom. Ten years ago, this church would have fallen under the label of the New Age Movement, but now it is simply one spiritual group among all the rest. Perhaps this is because the general decline of Christianity in Western cultures has left a spiritual void, or maybe it is what regularly comes around from time to time. In any case, the idea is gaining momentum that if people would drop their distinctive, exclusive beliefs there would be more harmony and peace. Wars and unrest involving religion in Ireland, Israel, Afghanistan and Iraq, to name just a few, reinforce society's desire to see a blending of religions. I suspect that the proliferation of indistinct and inclusive religious institutions will continue into the future. This is a natural development for those who think that all paths lead to God, or a goddess or some sort of higher power.

Arlo Guthrie, son of the Great Depression era folk singer Woody Guthrie, is headed in much the same direction as the group Gene Veith described in *World* magazine. In a *New York Times* article by Eric Goldschieder (5 January 2002), Guthrie is quoted as saying, 'I have three or four major traditions that I am carrying around inside me, and they are all just different views of the same reality.' Guthrie purchased a building that once housed a functioning church with the hope of transforming it into a trans-religious church. Guthrie will not be the last to do this and, in fact, I think it will catch on and spread rapidly, especially if such an enterprise proves economically viable.

## Jesus and the leaders of Israel

Jesus dealt directly with people who had been duped. He was not merely looking to build a large following. He was interested in neither money nor acceptance by the religious establishment. Jesus was concerned with correcting error and exposing hypocrisy through a presentation of the truth. Addressing the religious elite, Jesus said:

'Woe to you, scribes and Pharisees, hypocrites! for you build the tombs of the prophets and adorn the monuments of the righteous, saying, "If we had lived in the days of our fathers, we would not have taken part with them in shedding the blood of the prophets." Thus you witness against yourselves, that you are sons of those who murdered the prophets. Fill up, then, the measure of your fathers. You serpents, you brood of vipers, how are you to escape being sentenced to hell?' (Matt. 23:29–33).

It was well known that the predecessors of these leaders of Judaism had killed the prophets, had hounded them, persecuted them and attacked them in many ways. Read the stories of Elijah, Isaiah, Jeremiah and others, and you can see for yourself what happened. The great prophets had been rejected and even murdered by religious zealots. The people of Jesus' day said, 'We're not like those who killed the prophets.' They would beautify the prophet's tombs and make memorials to their name, but they did not believe in what the prophets had said about the coming Messiah. The prophets had clearly spoken of the Messiah and Jesus was fulfilling these prophecies perfectly. Yet the leaders were rejecting him. God had sent the last great prophet, John the Baptist, and John said of Jesus that he was 'the Lamb of God, who takes away the sin of the world' (John 1:29). John directly linked the prophecy of Isaiah 53 to Jesus, but the leaders of Israel consciously rejected his witness.

Everyone, from the least to the greatest in Israel, saw the miracles, the signs and the wonders that Jesus did, and they heard the message of the gospel from Jesus himself. Most of the religious leaders, however, steeled their hearts; they denied and rejected him. That is why Jesus said, 'You witness against yourself.' Then, in the most solemn part of his declaration, he said, 'How are you to escape being sentenced to hell?' Of course, the inference is: 'You will not escape.' And it is precisely because of the harsh reality of hell that we must confront error.

## Arrogance?

When Christians challenge belief systems, they run the risk of being charged with arrogance. 'Oh, so you have the truth, do you?' people will say. Additionally, we may be called 'narrow fundamentalists'. The idea is that we are very rigit in our beliefs and that we should be more tolerant and accepting. But we are not religious chameleons, believing whatever happens to be contemporary or the opinion of the majority. We believe that there is such a thing as absolute truth.

Christians can also be charged with not being loving. The love in question here is sentimental in nature, emotionally oriented, and characterized by the 'live and let live' view of life. From a biblical perspective, however, to sweep the gospel of Christ into the same box as all the rest of the world's religions is actually an unloving thing to do. Our only hope is in Jesus and the cross. To reduce Jesus to just another spiritual master would be to place him alongside all the false gods and goddesses that are powerless to rescue us from our sin. How loving would it be to let this go unchallenged? Love is shown by our concern for the ultimate fate of others. It would not be love if we were unconcerned for people who are on the road to hell. Christian love is expressed in presenting a way of escape.

## Reluctance to consider Jesus

I admit it can be a discomforting and difficult thing to consider the gospel of Jesus Christ. It is far simpler to ignore it all. This is what most people do — they simply ignore it. If you want to ignore Jesus, there is plenty of help around. There are many philosophical systems that aid and abet us in ignoring the gospel. Many groups exist, religious or secular, which lend support to ignoring or rejecting the message of Jesus altogether. Many of these are self-help groups, while others are spiritually-based groups that pay some homage to Jesus but essentially reject him. There are a number of groups that claim to have advanced knowledge and communications from celestial beings, angels or reincarnated spiritual masters, and they teach something far different from the Bible. These groups have a little bit of Jesus — a little truth — but the gospel message is distorted. The person who has been influenced by such teaching might well be hostile to a presentation of the gospel — at least he or she will be uncomfortable with it. It amounts to an unpleasant confrontation, but I plead with those who might find it easier to ignore Jesus and the gospel: pray that God would show you the truth, whatever that truth might be, even if it is Jesus. It is not sound judgement to reject something out of hand without testing it first. Jesus will let you test and try him; he will in fact invite it. You have nothing at all to lose and everything — and I do mean everything — to gain.

## The Jesus of major religious groups

Jesus is treated in an array of ways by other faiths. Obviously these treatments will not coincide with the dominant Christian view. This might be surprising to some who have imagined that all religions teach the same thing. No, Jesus is actually misrepresented by all the major religions and cults. If this were not so, they would not be distinct religions. In fact, the teachings about Jesus are at the very centre of the divergence. Most often, however, non-Christian groups transform Jesus into someone other than what both the Scripture says of him and what he has said about himself. I will not attempt to outline all the major points of doctrine for the following religious groups; instead, the focus will be strictly on their views of Jesus.

## Judaism

The various branches of Judaism, among which are the Orthodox, Conservative and Reformed branches, have done a remake of the Jesus of the New Testament — out of necessity. Since Judaism does not acknowledge Jesus as the Messiah, something had to be done to counter the claims of the early Christians. The early cover story was: 'Well, the disciples stole the body.' Matthew, perhaps hearing the account from Nicodemus or Joseph of Arimathea, both members of the ruling council who became believers in Jesus, described what happened:

> And when they had assembled with the elders and taken counsel, they gave a sum of money to the soldiers and said, 'Tell people, "His disciples came by night and stole him away while we were asleep." And if this comes to the governor's ears, we will satisfy him and keep you out of trouble.' So they took the money and did as they were directed; and this story has been spread among the Jews to this day (Matt. 28:12–15).

The spiritual leaders of Israel made a desperate attempt to prevent people from acknowledging Jesus as the Messiah. The result was an institutional rejection of the Messianic claims of Jesus. Any other response would have meant the end of their religion, as they knew it. It might have ended their careers as religious leaders — power, prestige and wealth would have been lost.

Many of the early converts to Christianity were Jews. Their own religious leaders had not persuaded them. Indeed, the denial of Jesus and his resurrection by the Jewish leadership meant that traditional Judaism would continue unabated instead of reaching its fulfilment in the Messiah. Paul, a Jew himself and rabbinically trained, said of those who were committed to the Law of Moses and Judaism, 'I bear them witness that they have a zeal for God, but it is not enlightened' (Rom. 10:2). Zeal and devotion are not proof of anything other than zeal and devotion. Suicide bombers have zeal and devotion. Anyone can be sincerely wrong. Over the centuries since the early church, many Jews have come to acknowledge Christ as their Saviour and Messiah (without losing their Jewish identity and heritage).

The counsel of Gamaliel, Paul's own rabbi and one of the truly great leaders of Israel, is startling. Gamaliel asserted that if the idea that Jesus is the resurrected Messiah were true then to oppose it would be to oppose God. He advised letting the Christians alone and then, if it were not from God, it would fail. Well, Christianity has not failed, but the Jews of that day and of this (I refer to official Judaism) reject the counsel of this first-century rabbi. Gamaliel actually went so far as to say, 'You might even be found opposing God!' (Read the account in Acts 5:33–39.) I appeal to every Jewish person: consider Jesus, study him and see if he is not the Messiah you are looking for.

## Eastern religions

Secondly, we turn to Hinduism, Buddhism and other religious philosophies that are based on them. Jesus has generally been reduced to just another spiritual master in these systems.

Hinduism is based on Monism, the philosophy that teaches that there is one reality and that there is no objective or separate reality. For the Monist, there is only the supreme deity, spirit, cosmic consciousness, mind, soul, and so on.

Monists, although they deny the reality of an objective world, must speak of it as though it were real anyway. (They use the term 'maya', or illusion, for the objective reality that the scientist examines and all human beings experience.) As contradictory as this might be, the Monist must somehow deal with Jesus. Their approach is that Jesus is another spiritual master, an avatar, or a great teacher. They add Christ to their pantheon of gods, but ultimately deny what the Scriptures reveal about Jesus and what Jesus said about himself. It appears to be a generous, tolerant acceptance.

A Hindu might endorse this statement: 'Jesus is your God. We'll believe in him, too.' This was Mahatma Gandhi's approach. He called himself a Hindu, a Muslim, a Jew, a Christian — meaning he thought they all worshipped the same God, but approached him in different ways. I under-stand this great man's attempt to reconcile various religions. Indeed, this ability to incorporate varying belief systems into Monistic thought is often treated as a strength, but it is essentially unfair and patronizing. I would rather have an out-and-out rejection of Jesus and Christianity than try to fit in with the Hindu mindset and establish an artificial common ground.

Hinduism claims to be the oldest religious tradition, but nothing is older than Judaism, and thus than Christianity. Moses wrote, or oversaw the writing of, the first five books of the Bible (the Pentateuch) in the middle of the second millennium before Christ. That easily makes these biblical books the oldest Scriptures in existence. Christianity is as old as Adam, and older in that the Scripture declares that Jesus died for us from before the foundation of the earth (1 Peter 1:20). But age is not the measure of truth — only something to remember as you consider the claims of the Bible.

Buddhism, which might be viewed as a reformation of Hinduism, owes its origin to Siddhartha Gautama, who was born about 563 B.C. in what is now Nepal. Gautama became known as the Enlightened One, or Buddha. Buddhism has many streams and is difficult to present briefly or simply. It has been described as a religion without a concept of a Creator God, but this is too simple to account for all the variations within Buddhism.

Gautama attempted to be free of all desire — for desire, he said, resulted in suffering. The goal was to reach Nirvana, a state of nothingness, or one in which the self does not experience suffering. The practice of Buddhism is said to lead to Enlightenment, an escape from reincarnation and an entrance into Nirvana, however that is defined.

Buddhists have treated Jesus in various ways; some have even viewed him as an enlightened one, a Buddha. This does not accurately represent Jesus at all, and effectively reduces him to an honoured spiritual master. The American Buddhists I have known tend to respect and reverence Jesus but would reject him as God in the flesh, who alone is the Saviour of the world.

Some within the general Christian community have tried to blend their faith with Buddhism. They do not necessarily hold to the Buddhist world view, but they appropriate meditation into a kind of interdisciplinary practice. Buddhism, however, sees suffering as the real evil and attempts to overcome it through the avoidance of any attachments, desires and cravings. Christianity, on the other hand, faces and accepts the reality of suffering. Jesus, for instance, suffered on the cross, willingly and purposefully. Jesus lived a real life in a real world and sent his disciples into the world to live in it and suffer in it. Jesus was not detached from the world or beyond it. He became flesh and dwelt in the world among its people, for its people. Jesus is not a Buddha who became enlightened; he is the eternal Son of God.

He did not teach *about* the truth; he proclaimed that he *is* the truth. He did not die peacefully, surrounded by his friends, like Gautama, but he died alone and violently.

## Islam

We turn next to Islam. It is the major world religion that is connected to both Judaism and Christianity.

Muslims teach that Jesus really did not die on the cross at all. Thus, the central point of Christianity, the sacrifice for sin by God himself, is denied. Islam teaches that Judas died on the cross and not Jesus. This is the heart of it and this is the testimony of the Qur'an and the prophet Mohammed. According to Islam, Jesus did not atone for sin and he is not God in any way, form or sense. They revere Jesus, but believe that Mohammed replaced and superseded him. The Jesus of Islam becomes just another religious figure on a par with Noah, Abraham, Moses and David.

According to Muslims Jesus is a great religious figure, but this Jesus is one of their own making. Muslims must reject what the Bible teaches about Jesus or they would have to reject the major tenets of their own religion. The two cannot coexist. Islam's version of Jesus reduces him to just another spiritual master.

## Cults with Christian links

There are a number of groups that owe their origins to Christianity but, somewhere along the line, have developed doctrines that deviate to such an extent from those of mainstream Christianity that they can no longer be called orthodox Christian denominations. It may sound harsh to describe such groups as 'cults', but we fool ourselves if we neglect the importance of doctrine. Historic Christianity, without apology, uses the term 'cult' to designate those teachings that are antithetical to an orthodox theology.

Cults with Christian links have an even stronger interest in twisting the biblical view of the person and work of Jesus than do the major world religions. When I use the term 'cults' to describe such people, I do not do it with any rancour, because I always hope that there will be adjustment in their theology. We have seen this happen. In my lifetime, we have seen members of two groups previously classified as cults change their theology for the better — when any group reveres and studies the Bible, there is the potential for change. We saw it with some members of the Worldwide Church of God who turned away from divergent doctrine and embraced orthodox, biblical Christianity, and now there are those within the Seventh Day Adventists who have also moved away from doctrines that separated them from the broader Christian community.

## Mormonism

God, for the Mormon, was once like any man, flesh and bones, but achieved the status of deity. Through good works, a Mormon can potentially achieve godhood. The Mormon god is ever progressing, as any human being might, in knowledge and power. Mormonism rejects the Trinity and views the Father, Son and Holy Spirit as three separate and distinct gods. Their version of God the Father is a polygamous, former male earthling who is believed to have eternal wives through whom he produces spirit children. Christ is thought to be the first of these children born to God, and Satan, or Lucifer, was originally the spirit brother of Christ. One of the most bizarre Mormon doctrines is that God the Father had actual sexual relations with Mary that resulted in the conception of Jesus.

The Mormon ideas of humankind are interesting, too. According to Mormon doctrine, humans were never created but are eternal as God is. It is easy to understand, then, that in their system people can become gods.

In Mormon terms, salvation comes only through compliance with the rites, rituals, and doctrines of the Mormon church. Here is their most obvious cultic component. Mormons do not refer to Jesus as just another spiritual master, but their treatment of him amounts to about the same thing. Jesus is not the Saviour, rather the Mormon church is. Thus, the death of Jesus on the cross and his resurrection are presented far differently from how the Bible presents them.

## Jehovah's Witnesses

I have hope for Jehovah's Witnesses. They are running out of options; they really have their backs up against the wall. Their prophecies are over-due; some are long past due.

Jehovah's Witnesses diligently study the Bible and energetically pursue their religion, but they too deny the biblical Jesus. They make something strange of Jesus so that they can insert the Watchtower Society into the place the Saviour should occupy. This is the same process used by Islam and Mormonism.

The Witnesses have transformed Jesus into essentially just another spiritual master. They teach that Jesus was the incarnation of Michael the archangel and that Jesus resumed the name Michael when he returned to heaven at the ascension. Instead of Jesus being the Saviour, the organization itself becomes the saviour. And the organization is not much of a saviour, either. Only 144,000, according to their notion, will go to heaven. This is the anointed class, the little flock — the rest must spend eternity on a restored paradise earth. But even to be able to make it to paradise is no easy undertaking and involves being an approved and faithful member of the Watchtower Society. For the Jehovah's Witness, instead of being the Redeemer, Lord and King, Jesus is reduced to merely angelic status.

## Too many to mention

There is not space to mention the dozens of other groups that have done a makeover on Jesus. Among the cults with Christian roots, there is Christian Science, which is really a Hindu version of Christianity. The Course in Miracles is similar to Christian Science and is monistic like Hinduism. Then there are groups like Science of Mind, Religious Science, Urantia, Bahai and Unity, which have made Jesus into nothing more than just another spiritual master. They appeal to those who have rejected biblical Christianity but are attracted to spirituality and philosophy. The Jesus espoused by these groups is anaemic, ineffectual and mystical — not the Lord of lords and King of kings as Scripture attests.

## Liberal Christianity

Christianity runs the gamut from fundamentalist to liberal. Fundamentalism may go a bit overboard sometimes, but the Jesus of the fundamentalist is still biblical and orthodox. The same cannot always be said for those on the liberal end of the Christian spectrum. For many liberals, Jesus has been stripped of his deity, uniqueness and saving power and has become little more than a great teacher or prophet who taught sacrifice, love and compassion. The result is not very different from the Jesus presented by the Hindu or Buddhist.

## What really matters

It makes little difference who does what with Jesus and the Scripture if Jesus ends up as just another spiritual master. A deception and distortion of truth have occurred and this is the issue. I am neither shocked nor offended about the distortions of Jesus, but my hope is to set the record straight so that those who have been duped might see who Jesus really is.

## The biblical record: The witness of John

Consider John 1:1–3. These verses remind us of the opening verses of Genesis. John writes, 'In the beginning was the Word, and the Word was with God, and the Word was God.' 'Word' is the translation of the Greek word *logos*. A later verse shows that John is referring to Jesus when he says *logos*: 'And the Word became flesh and dwelt among us, full of grace and truth; we have beheld his glory, glory as of the only Son of the Father' (John 1:14). John's use of the word 'only' refers to Christ's uniqueness — there is no one like him.

'In the beginning' means before the creation of the world; there was not an atom, not a second, only God. John testifies that God the Son — Jesus — was there, was with God and was God. The word 'was' is probably the best English word to render the Greek term. But in English, it is past tense and may give the notion, however illogical, that the *logos* is not God now, present tense. In Greek grammar, *logos* is a verb of being (an imperfect) and does not imply time at all. It is best to say he 'was and is'. Think of it. How could God not be God now if he was God before? The *logos*, Jesus, was and is God, past, present and future. This expresses who Jesus is. He is God.

There has been a tendency in some cults and sects to say that Jesus was created, that there was a time when he was not — making Jesus a lesser god. Gnostics did this; Jesus for them was in a sense divine but not really the ultimate God. Gnostics were the forerunners of those who mistakenly suppose Jesus is simply another divinely inspired teacher. But John's witness makes this impossible. And John clearly is interpreting what the Old Testament prophets had already said about the Messiah. You can read Isaiah 7:14 and Isaiah 9:16, for example, to see this. John did not decide that Jesus must be God. John knew the Old Testament and he had seen and heard Jesus. John knew who Jesus was.

John 1:2 reads, 'He was in the beginning with God.' The idea expressed is that the Father and the Son had, and have, the same nature and the same will. It is not so much that the Father and the Son were together in the same space as that the Father and Son are of the same substance and nature and will.

In verse 3 we see that through Jesus the universe was created. 'All things were made through him and without him was not anything made that was made.' Certainly the concept of the Trinity is a great mystery. The Trinity is the doctrine that the three, God the Father, God the Son and God the Holy Spirit, are one. I would not believe this unless the biblical witness compelled me to. The fact of the Trinity is to be clearly seen in the Scripture — an accurate rendering of the evidence. The biblical view of the nature of God is that the Father created the universe *through* the Son *by* the power of the Holy Spirit (Gen. 1:2). By 'through' the Gospel writer means 'in conjunction with' and 'for'. It is difficult to understand, but the point John is making is that Jesus is God.

Verse 14, quoted earlier, succinctly tells the story of the incarnation — the *logos* became flesh. Of course, this is the story of Christmas; this introduces us to the great paradox of Jesus — he is both God and man simultaneously. It is essential to understand why this is so important. The overriding human problem is sin — our individual sin. Our sin separates us from God and we are incapable of bridging that gap. God, in Christ, atones for and covers our sin by becoming the sacrifice. Only God is holy and only God can be the perfect sacrifice. But sacrifice means death, and since God cannot die, God became man so that he might actually die for us. Jesus then, fully God and fully man, could be the perfect sacrifice for our sin. He must be God and he must be man. He was and is both God and man, but we cannot comprehend it fully. We see it, we understand the necessity of it, but we cannot fully grasp it. Perhaps this is why we must have faith to come to Jesus in the first place.

## The biblical record: The witness of Paul

We will now examine Colossians 1:15–20. This passage is Paul's explanation of Jesus' nature. Whatever your background might be, it is always difficult to have an accurate understanding of who Jesus really is. But when you see who he is, you will see why it is that world religions and cults which deviate from the Bible must diminish and distort him.

Paul writes in Colossians 1:15: 'He is the image of the invisible God, the first-born of all creation.' Paul means that when you have seen Jesus, you have seen God; when you believe in Jesus, you believe in God.

'First-born' is a word that means 'head of' or 'over'. The reason why Jesus is head of or ruler of all creation is found in the following verse: 'For in him all things were created, in heaven and on earth, visible and invisible, whether thrones or dominions or principalities or authorities — all things were created through him and for him' (Col. 1:16). Jesus is both Lord and King.

Paul continues, 'He is before all things, and in him all things hold together' (Col. 1:17). Jesus is supreme: he is before all things and in him they hold together. Who keeps the world, both organic and inorganic, from spinning off into chaos? Jesus does.

The following verse tells us that 'He is the head of the body, the church; he is the beginning, the first-born from the dead, that in everything he might be pre-eminent' (Col. 1:18). Jesus is Lord of the church (those who belong to him by faith). Jesus, the first to be raised incorruptible from the dead, is Lord of the dead. Jesus is pre-eminent; he is the first-born, the Alpha and the Omega, the Sovereign Lord.

Is it any mystery, then, why so many, for so long, have been intent on making Jesus out to be just another spiritual master? If what the Old Testament prophets, Jesus himself and the apostolic witnesses said is true, then the religions of the world and cults which deviate from the Bible are false. They must reduce, distort and twist Jesus to fit him into their own versions of truth. I would rather they would reject the truth of who Jesus is out-right. Instead, they attempt a makeover. They pretend to embrace Jesus but really flatter, equivocate, mince words and in the end concoct a religious figure who is impotent and forlorn. It is inaccurate and blatantly dishonest.

Paul continues, 'For in him all the fulness of God was pleased to dwell, and through him to reconcile to himself all things, whether on earth or in heaven, making peace by the blood of his cross' (Col. 1:19–20). Now we come to the important part. Notice Paul's words: 'and through him to reconcile to himself all things.' Only God can do that — reconcile, or bring back. In order to be reconciled with God, our sins must be forgiven. This is why Jesus went to the cross and took our sins upon himself. In Christ, God graciously forgives and restores us and brings us back into relationship with him. This is why we speak of grace. Grace means that, since we cannot forgive our own sin or do anything that might earn forgiveness, God forgives us through Christ and brings us back into fellowship with him — all his own doing.

Clearly, we see that if Jesus is not God in the flesh, then of course he is no more than a good example; he is no more than a good teacher; he is no more than a prophet; he is no more than a spiritual master. You can easily dismiss Jesus once you take away his deity, his supremacy and his lordship. The religions of the world attack the biblical view of Jesus because *if he is God then what he did on the cross is the most important thing that has ever happened.*

## Conclusion

Who do you think Jesus is? What is it that he did? If you diminish Jesus, he will just be there in history as a grand figure who stands along with many other great prophets and religious leaders. But once you see and acknowledge who he is, you realize you are not finished with him because he has promised to come again. He will come back and he will stand on the last day as Judge of the living and the dead. Do you see the danger of diminishing, distorting and perverting who Jesus is? You might be tempted to think that you have done away with him but, make no mistake about it, he will return.

Many will hear Jesus say on the last day, 'I never knew you; depart from me you evildoers' (Matt. 7:23). You dare not dismiss this God. I challenge those who have been deceived into believing in the Jesus presented by a world religion or a cult — you have been duped if you have fallen for a Jesus you think you will not have to meet face to face. Do not lose everything, even your eternal life, by thinking that Jesus is anyone other than who the Scriptures say he is.

# CHAPTER 9

# You have been duped if you think you are a Christian but you do not love Jesus

M y concern is that there are those readers who suppose or presume that they are Christians but are not. Many have been deceived on this most crucial issue — it is more common than you might think. It is not a judgement on my part for I do not know if you are a genuine Christian or not. But you must examine yourself to see whether you truly love Jesus Christ.

Many have some idea of Christianity, especially in Western cultures. Many who are born in America, Britain, or any of the European Union nations, Russia and so on, have a Protestant, Catholic or Orthodox background, but that is not the same as being a real Christian. Many are raised in a Christian home and yet remain unconverted. You may be infused with Christian principles and saturated with Christian ideals, but that does not make you a Christian.

## False conversion

How easy it is to experience a false conversion! Since I began working on the nature of conversion in 1997, I had no idea of all I would discover. And I have to say that the problem of false conversion may be greater now than in earlier periods in history.

The rise in false conversions is partly due to the panic in evangelical Christianity to get people into the pews. I say 'panic' because it does not seem enough to many pastors and preachers simply to present the gospel of Christ and depend on the Holy Spirit to do the work of converting.

Relying on 'techniques' to get people to become Christians often results in Christianization, or false conversion, rather than genuine conversion.

Christianity has been in decline in America and Europe for some time and consequently there have been tremendous resources put into attracting the 'unchurched'. Although such efforts appear to have been successful, there has not been a net gain in the number of Christians in America and Britain. Indeed, only a recycling of Christians has occurred — a shuffling around from one church to another. Telemarketing experts have discovered what activities, music and theologies attract people. Through the use of sophisticated packaging strategies, small-group dynamics, bonding processes and music presentations that are able to stimulate the emotions, some churches have been able to attract new members. But is this the same as true conversion to Christ? Are people coming into these churches for sociological and psychological reasons? My experience tells me, yes, they are. It is to these people I want to direct this chapter.

## Not so new

I have been rereading through one of the greatest books ever written for preachers — *Preaching and Preachers* by D. Martyn Lloyd-Jones (Zondervan, 1972). I hope to read it once a year. It is a transcription of a series of sermons from a conference for preachers held during the mid-1960s. Lloyd-Jones addressed the issue of false conversion because he observed the use of some questionable techniques that were being employed to get people into the pews. Lloyd-Jones was already seeing, even at that time, the beginning of the problem. At that time, there was a growing acceptance of certain forms of music and worship that he felt would mislead people and attract them to a church for the wrong reasons. So he sounded the alarm and said, 'Look, people are going to come for just this alone. You do not have to preach any kind of biblical gospel message. You can simply fill up the pews using these techniques' (the author's summary of Lloyd-Jones' argument). Lloyd-Jones said these things in the mid-1960s but these sermons could easily have been preached in the mid-1990s or early 2000s.

## 'Christian lite'

I am appalled when I see psychological bonding processes used to bring people into churches. I cringe when I read these ploys in advertisements I receive in the mail. The appeal is that through the small-group bonding process people will sign up, join up and even pledge to give money for the capital funds campaign. There is nothing wrong with small groups — we have them at Miller Avenue — but a person can make a commitment to a group and not to Christ. When I express my frustration with such schemes, some question me, 'What is the matter? If it works to get people into the church building at least they will be in a place where they will hear the gospel.' That would be fine if that were so and they heard the gospel. But there is usually not much of a true gospel preached in those settings because the gospel is bound to offend. My experience has been that the Christianity in these churches is what I call 'Christian lite' — just enough Christianity to mollify most people, but not enough to bring a person face-to-face with the person and work of Jesus Christ. A little moralizing, some sad, heart-warming story about a dog or a child, with maybe a little patriotism thrown in — a few tears are shed, and that is the end of it. The real problem with 'Christian lite' is that it produces counterfeit conversion.

## Meeting human need

Christians should reach out to people who are in need. We are interested, and legitimately so, in enhancing people's lives, alleviating suffering and being advocates for the unjustly accused. This is one of the reasons that I have been a long-time volunteer at San Quentin Prison. This is why our Miller Avenue church has conducted seventy eight-week divorce recovery workshops over the last eighteen years and why we are into our sixth year of holding Saturday lunches for the homeless in our community.

We reach out to help other people, yet if our helping is not done properly it can result in false conversions. People in need will gravitate towards that which benefits them and they may adopt the general viewpoints of the benefactors — uncritically. This simply contributes to the problem of false conversion. The disadvantaged, immigrants and the poor are often target groups for church outreach. And, if properly funded and staffed, such efforts will usually be successful in terms of people being recruited. People may indeed be helped on one level, but the greater issue is genuine reconciliation with God.

There is a major non-Christian world religion now growing rapidly in America that targets poor communities. If you adopt this religion, you may find a great deal of assistance available. I wonder what is really going on — are people coming to it because they are being helped financially, education-ally or socially? Of course, that is exactly what is happening. Christians have to be careful not to package their ministries in the same way.

In the late 1960s, I was a street preacher in San Francisco's Haight-Ashbury district. Hippie kids from all over America ended up there. For a few months, I lived in a storefront mission in the Fillmore, a neighbourhood near the Haight. I saw first-hand what desperate people would do to survive — we had many converts at the evening meetings, which preceded dinnertime. Many 'salvation' prayers were said just before the food was served and many repeated the same prayers the next night and the next. I soon realized that I had these people eating out of my hand, almost literally. I have seen the same thing at the prison — convicts signing up for the chapel programmes for reasons other than a genuine interest in Jesus.

## There is more

People will also think they are Christians because they have been baptized. People think they are converted if they are members of a church, or if they are simply loving or merciful or positive people. People think they are converted if they prayed a model prayer at some point. People think they are converted if they simply believe in God — that is, they are not atheist or agnostic. I am reminded of what James said: 'You believe that God is one; you do well. Even the demons believe — and shudder' (James 2:19). Some will think they are converted if they ascribe to a Christian creed such as the Apostles' Creed. Many Christian observers would call this doctrinal salvation — basing conversion on the acceptance of orthodox doctrine.

Some think they are Christians because they have had spiritual experiences. You might be surprised at what I am about to say, but I think it is an important enough topic for me to risk being misunderstood. I have come to this after my experience in the Jesus Movement, the Charismatic and Pentecostal movements and after reading about the dark side of some of the great revivals of history, including the First and Second Great Awakenings in America. If you want spiritual experiences, you will get them. Now, I do not mean experiences of the Holy Spirit of God; I mean simply spiritual experiences. Is the devil not a spiritual being who can disguise himself as an angel of light? Are not demons spiritual? If you wait for a 'spirit' to come to you, it could happen. If you wait to hear the voice of God or to be touched by an angel, it is very possible that you will hear a voice or be touched. But it might not be God — rather something else, something unholy and dangerous.

It is entirely possible to have a spiritual experience that is so dramatic and concrete that it removes any doubt concerning the existence of the supernatural. Having such an experience does not demonstrate conversion at all, but many are deceived in this manner.

I want to say something now as carefully as I can. You might even have a spiritual experience that is from the Holy Spirit, or you might witness a genuine miracle wrought by the Holy Spirit, but that does not mean you have been converted. I have known people who have witnessed such miracles and who then concluded that they must be converted or they would not have been allowed to witness the miraculous. Certainly many people saw the miracles of Jesus but never came to trust him as their Saviour. There are numerous examples in the Scriptures to prove this point.

## Jesus and 'spiritual' people

I want to remind you that Jesus confronted people who felt they were 'in with God' because of their spirituality. Luke 4 records the story of a visit Jesus made to his home town, Nazareth. He attended a service at the local synagogue, perhaps the one he had grown up in. The synagogue attendant invited Jesus to read the portion of Scripture from the Prophets, a standard component of the synagogue service. Jesus complied and read from the scroll of the prophet Isaiah. He read, 'The Spirit of the Lord is upon me, because he has anointed me to preach good news to the poor. He has sent me to proclaim release to the captives and recovering of sight to the blind, to set at liberty those who are oppressed, to proclaim the acceptable year of the Lord' (Luke 4:18–19; see also Isa. 61:1–2). After returning the scroll of Isaiah to the attendant, Jesus said, 'Today this scripture has been fulfilled in your hearing' (Luke 4:21).

But there were no great works, or miracles, done in Nazareth. The people expected Jesus to do miracles in his home town, but he did not. In nearby Capernaum, Jesus had healed people, and those in Nazareth knew it and they wondered why he did not do so there. Jesus replied, 'Truly, I say to you, no prophet is acceptable in his own country' (Luke 4:24).

As I see it, the people of Nazareth had two problems. Firstly, they did not see their spiritual need; they were blinded by their own righteousness. This led to their second problem: they held Jesus to be ordinary, like the young man they had known, the son of Mary and Joseph. It was as though they said, 'We know your parents; we know your family; you are nobody special.'

Jesus, in dealing with his former neighbours, told them two stories: one about Elijah and one about Elisha. We find these stories in the Old Testament in 1 and 2 Kings. In the ninth century before Christ, the great prophet of

Israel was Elijah. The region was enduring a tremendous famine, which lasted for three years. God sent Elijah out of Israel over to the Mediterranean coast to an area called Syro-Phoenicia. Elijah went to a poor woman who had a young son, and he lodged with this non-Jewish family and provided for their needs. After the young boy died he was miraculously raised from the dead through Elijah's ministry.

The second story Jesus told was about Elisha, the successor of Elijah. Again, the central figure was a non-Jew, a military commander whose nation of Syria often warred with Israel. Naaman, had leprosy, but there was a young Jewish girl, a captive, in Naaman's household who said, and I paraphrase, 'I know somebody that could take care of your leprosy problem.' The Syrian military leader came to Elisha, the Jewish prophet, and was healed of his leprosy.

Jesus told these stories in the synagogue of Nazareth. And do you know what happened? Luke records their response: 'When they heard this, all in the synagogue were filled with wrath. And they rose up and put him out of the city, and led him to the brow of the hill on which their city was built, that they might throw him down headlong' (Luke 4:28–29).

Jesus appeared to be rejecting his own people when he said that God would favour non-Jews. The racial and religious pride of the people of Nazareth was stirred up and they tried to kill Jesus. However, as verse 30 reveals, 'passing through the midst of them he went away.'

Jesus knew their problem; he knew why the Holy Spirit had not been poured out upon them. These descendants of Abraham, Isaac and Jacob, these people who had the law of Moses and worshipped at the temple in Jerusalem, were smug and secure in their righteousness. By virtue of their race and religious heritage, they thought they were 'in with God'.

As I already mentioned, these people held Jesus to be ordinary and common; they did not see who he really was. So they despised him and tried to kill him. This is the story of the people of Nazareth, but it is also the story of us all. They did not love him; they hated him — and we have been duped if we think we are accepted by God but do not love Jesus.

## The text: John 8:42

John 8 records the story of a confrontation Jesus had with people who thought they had a relationship with God. The situation is somewhat like the people of Nazareth in Luke 4. The difference is that in John 8 the people Jesus was debating with were religious professionals. Jesus said to them, 'If God were your Father, you would love me' (John 8:42).

Very direct and to the point, isn't it? Of course, the title of this chapter is based on this verse, and I think it provides the quickest way to test for genuine conversion. 'If you have a relationship with God, then, you will love me.' Love for Jesus is the issue. If they had a relationship with God, as they claimed, then they would have recognized Jesus to be the Messiah they had been looking for.

By the way, do you see the 'if' in our passage? According to the rules of Greek grammar this version of 'if' means, 'If God were your Father, and *he is not...*' Those who heard Jesus' words would have known that he did not believe God was their Father. Jesus literally said, 'God is not your Father as you claim.' It is not vague in the Greek. On the basis of their Jewishness, and more especially on the basis of their careful religious observances, they were boasting: 'Abraham is our father; God is our Father; how dare you challenge us?'

The implications are staggering. 'If God were your Father, you would love me.' This must always be the line drawn in the sand. There are many lines scratched out in the sand these days, but this is the ultimate line, greater than anything that any president or emperor or dictator, or anyone else in the history of the world, has ever drawn. Imagine Jesus saying it to you, 'If God were your Father, you would love me.'

## What is this love about?

Consider this question: 'What does it mean to love Jesus?'

The apostle Peter helps answer this question: 'Without having seen him you love him; though you do not now see him you believe in him and rejoice with unutterable and exalted joy' (1 Peter 1:8). The connection between love and faith is clear. Peter had known Jesus personally, while the people to whom Peter wrote this letter had not. Peter had even heard Jesus ask him, 'Simon, son of John, do you love me?' (John 21:16). Peter had been able to say that he did, but the recipients of Peter's letter had no such opportunity. So Peter links faith and love. Peter has more to say, though — he speaks of rejoicing and joy. This joy is the outcome of faith and love. Is joy not an integral part of love? To rejoice in the beloved — this is indeed sweet, pure love. Surely then we will know whether we have a love for Jesus or not.

## Jesus is 'sweet'

After I became a Christian I would occasionally run across the word 'sweet' when singing hymns. The grand old hymn 'Tis so sweet to trust in Jesus', written by Priscilla Owens, is an example. I wondered about the word being applied to God. In the hymn book we use at Miller Avenue, the word pops up in many hymns. There are also other words and phrases that are used to describe love for Jesus that have an almost romantic sound to them.

The word 'sweet' was used by the Puritans in describing how they felt about Jesus. They meant that Jesus and the things of the gospel had become precious to them. Before their conversion, either Jesus meant nothing to them or they despised him. But that all changed. Jesus and the gospel became sweet. This is always the case.

I do not use the word myself and when I have heard it, and others like it, I am rather startled. But I know what is meant and upon reflection I will say to myself, 'Yes, Jesus is sweet.'

## *Agape* love

In Greek, there are a number of different words for love. The word under consideration here is *agape*. In general, *agape* love is not a love we have by virtue of our humanness. We are capable on our own of having *phileo* love — brotherly or familial love. And we are also capable of having *eros* — passionate, even erotic or sensual love, whether it is for music, art, nature, or another person. These loves are possible because of who we are as human beings. But *agape* love is not acquirable or naturally attainable by human beings. It is a love that is given and that is what you have to see here. If we claim that we know God, that we have a relationship with him, then we will have *agape* for Jesus. The apostle John put it this way, 'In this is love, not that we loved God but that he loved us' (1 John 4:10). *Agape* love is the love God has for us. *Agape* love for God is a love God gives to us. It is given and it begins to grow in us when we are born again.

## An analogy

Normally children learn to trust and love their parents. It is one of the strongest of earthly loves. It is a tremendous love. Observe now the parallel. When we are born again, a trust in and love for God begin to grow. This is every bit as natural as parent/child love is. This love for God produces the desire to be close to him. It gives us the sense of wanting to spend time with the object of our love. I have often observed that converted people want to spend time with the Lord. They want to read the Bible, to pray and to know more about Jesus. They even desire to praise and worship God — these are concrete expressions of loving God.

There is also a hunger for God. Sometimes it is so strong that it seems as if we cannot be filled up. This hunger for God is the *agape* type of love that Jesus, John and Peter referred to. Some have hated God, despised him, ignored him and cursed his name, but all that changed after they were converted.

Genuine Christians also love to hear the gospel preached — even if they hated it before their conversion. Though we may have heard it a thousand times, yet we still love to hear the gospel preached. It is such a strange thing, isn't it? Regular people, sinners though we are, reading the Bible, praying, worshipping and praising God, perhaps listening to some old preacher like me on Sunday morning, putting money into the offering plate and denying ourselves — this is because of *agape* love for God. And if it is not there — if these things are not in your life — you must question whether you have a relationship with God or not.

## Why love Jesus?

'Out of the ivory palaces' is a phrase that comes from the hymn 'Ivory Palaces'. George Beverly Shea used to sing it at Billy Graham crusades. It tells the story of Jesus. 'Out of the ivory palaces into a world of woe' — God himself became flesh and dwelt among us. Paul taught that Jesus emptied himself, took the form of a servant, and became obedient unto death. Knowing what was going to come next, knowing that our sin would be laid upon him, still he came to be with us. He took our sin, our judgement, our condemnation, and our hell upon himself. He physically died and suffered in that way for us. More than that, he died spiritually, for even fellowship with the Father was broken. This is why Jesus cried out on the cross, 'Father, why have you forsaken me?'

This is quite personal. Did Jesus die for you personally? John 3:16, reads in part, 'For God so loved the world...' When you know Jesus, you have the sense that he loved you *specifically*. You can say, 'For God so loved [your name].'

Consider again that Jesus did this *for us* — lawbreakers and sinners. Consider also what he said on the cross: 'Father, forgive them; for they know not what they do' (Luke 23:34). I love that verse. There was no vengeance, bitterness, anger or resentment on the part of Jesus. We do not know what we are doing — rebellious, ignorant sinners that we are. But consider his great love for us, his forgiving us, his saving us, and his promise to come back for us because he wants us to be with him.

## The question

Let me close the chapter with this challenge. This is a question you must not avoid; this is a question to which you must not give an easy answer. *Do you love Jesus?* If not, you should not consider yourself a Christian. If you think you are a Christian and you do not have love for Jesus, how is it that you could be a Christian? I can find no clearer way to challenge you.

Loving Jesus means believing in him, obeying him, following him, desiring to please him, studying him, and so much more. We know that love in the human sense is usually emotionally based. Loving Jesus is not emotional, though it may include that, but has to do with the will and the spirit. Jesus becomes foremost for the Christian; he is the centre, the foundation and the joy of living. Love for Jesus is beyond my ability to communicate.

It is my hope to present the gospel in such a way that those for whom Jesus died should come to him and be forgiven. I know that it is scary to examine yourself in such a blunt way. If you realize that you do not love Jesus, it is not too late. Seek him, look to him — he will receive you. If you see that you do love Jesus, then there is great assurance. If you love Jesus, you can know that you belong to him and he belongs to you.

You know whether you love Jesus or not. If you do, there will be a desire to praise and to worship him, a desire to follow him and be like him — and so much more. 'If God were your Father,' Jesus said, 'you would love me.' As hard as it is, I have to direct this question to you again: *Do you love Jesus?*

# CHAPTER 10

# You have been duped if you think being very religious earns points with God

Some may think the title of this chapter is inappropriate or inaccurate. Should not the very religious person be congratulated? You may think so, but my understanding of the matter, the understanding of the apostle Paul, and that of Jesus himself, is otherwise.

Jesus was not impressed by the very religious. For example, Nicodemus, a Pharisee and member of the ruling council of Israel, was no doubt as spiritual as you or I could be; yet Jesus told him he had to be born again (John 3:3). Ironically, during the ministry of Jesus, it was the scribes, Pharisees and Sadducees — the religious leaders of Israel — who conspired against him. They already had all they needed in their own rituals and traditions.

The very religious of any age have little genuine interest in Jesus. Why would they need or want Jesus anyway? The non-religious, the sinners, were attracted to Jesus during his earthly ministry, and it is the same today. Those who realize they cannot earn God's favour are attracted to Jesus and the message of the gospel.

Excessive religiosity may be a substitute or a counterfeit for genuine conversion. At times, I have thought that extreme religious expressions and lifestyles might be symptomatic of an obsessive-compulsive disorder whereby a person is attempting to control his or her anxiety through religious observances and rituals. Over the course of three decades in the pastoral ministry, I have observed this many times. At first, it is impressive, the seeming faithful devotion, but the favourable early impression often turns to dismay or even alarm.

I have in mind religious extremists who blow themselves, and others, up in the name of God. I also have in mind people who are driven by a sense of guilt and shame to try to achieve peace and forgiveness through 'religious' acts. They might mutilate themselves, punish themselves — severely deprive themselves of normal creature comforts — all with the mistaken notion that to do so will earn them forgiveness. Every form of religion rewards, even promotes, this type of behaviour, sometimes including Christianity. When Christian groups encourage a theology of 'works', extreme devotion may be expected. We see this in those who, in the name of religion, kill abortion doctors. Members of Christian Identity, a quasi Christian/political organization, plot to overthrow the United States government through terrorism. In the past decade I have had members of radical groups, who engage in murderous, criminal activity, attempt to infiltrate Miller Avenue Baptist Church. So, I have had first-hand experience with the twisting power of religiously based ideologies. My point is that such people will imagine themselves to be actual, born-again Christians.

## 'Religion lite'

Another counterfeit for the real thing is what I call 'religion lite'. Although I am addressing the very religious in this chapter, I want to briefly mention the opposite end of the spectrum — the nominal Christian.

Are you a nominal Christian? That is, are you a Christian in name only? It happens mostly with people who were born into a sacramental church, a church that practises infant baptism. The idea is that the church confers Christian graces upon a person through rites and ceremonies. Nominal Christians may assume they were born Christian and that is the end of it. Out of fear, obligation, or a desire to please family members, the nominal Christian will periodically show up at church and participate in communion, confession or an Easter or Christmas service. They actually know little of the Bible or the doctrines of their church and would be reluctant to identify themselves as Christians to their peers. If you are a nominal Christian, you have been duped every bit as much as the overly religious person.

## The purpose of this chapter

Can you see the difference between religion and grace? The concept is not easy to describe, but with the help of a passage in Acts, we will see that there is a marked distinction between the very religious and those who rely solely on Jesus Christ. But first, some remarks on religion in general.

# Religion is universal

Human beings are religious. How many hundreds of millions are Buddhists? How many hundreds of millions are Hindus? How many hundreds of millions are Muslim? How many hundreds of millions are Christian? It has been this way for centuries and even, in some cases, millenniums. From the dawn of human history, before any organized religions existed, anthropologists have found elaborate burial plots which indicate that religious belief systems were already in place. Human beings have always been quite religious.

Of course there are atheists and agnostics, but in fact being an atheist or an agnostic is just another belief system — he or she follows a religion. Atheism takes both faith and work; it takes convincing; it demands a continual affirmation that there is no God. Agnostics must work even harder than atheists since they believe God cannot be known. Imagine the necessity of acquiring and accessing encyclopedic knowledge and then determining that none of it pointed to the existence of a God. Surely, this would be a most daunting endeavour. However, if I were not a Christian, I suppose that I would be either an atheist or an agnostic. And, like everyone else, I would make a religion out of that.

To me religious trappings, and religion itself, have been unappealing. I am fortunate in that the smells, sounds and sights of religion do not easily captivate me. I do not care for the vestments, incense, bells, whistles, and all that goes along with the more elaborate forms of Christianity. (Others are not bothered by these things and I do not mean to cast disparagement on those who are so attracted.) But I have observed to what extremes religion itself can take you — it can give the false impression of personal righteousness on the one hand and, on the other, the impression that ornamental displays orchestrated by grand institutions are evidence of the authenticity of that institution.

Many people claim that if it were not for religion, there would be few wars. I disagree with that assessment because most wars are between nations, not religions. Consider Adolf Hitler. He was of no particular religion; if anything, he was enchanted by astrology and a supremacist, racist philosophy. Joseph Stalin, Chairman Mao, Pol Pot — they were all atheists, but they made communism into a religion. Many wars that people perceive as religious in nature were actually politically motivated. Sometimes there is a combination of things — the intertwining of the religious and the political — as we are seeing in Northern Ireland. Politicians always hope to have the dominant religion in their corner, whether they are believers or not. This further complicates the picture. Still, there is no question that religion has played a role in the warfare of the world.

Today, in the so-called 'War on Terrorism', political leaders in America say, 'It is not America versus Islam.' Americans do not want to believe that this war is Islam versus 'Christian' America. Some of us have another perspective. We wonder how large a role the teachings of the Qur'an and the proclamations of certain Muslim clerics play in all of this. Is it really just political, or is it religious to some degree as well?

Why are people so attracted to religion? I suppose there is the desire to make sense of our world, to understand our existence, to come to grips with life and, more particularly, to come to grips with death. Religious ideas do seem to soften the harsh realities of life and death. Even during the early Christian era, the philosophically oriented Greeks of the ancient city of Athens were seriously inclined towards religion.

## The text: Acts 17:16–27

During Paul's second missionary journey, he entered alone into the Greek city of Athens. Athens — that renowned, wealthy and ancient city — did not have the grandeur that it once had, say six hundred years previously. In Paul's day, it was still a gathering place for intellectuals and philosophers, a centre of the arts, and a very religious city.

## Paul's own religious experience

Luke, the author of Acts, records: 'Now while Paul was waiting for them at Athens, his spirit was provoked within him as he saw that the city was full of idols' (Acts 17:16). Some ancient writer had said that there were more gods in Athens than there were people. Whether they took their idols seriously or not is unknown, but they took them seriously enough to support a host of them. There were the idols, and there were the shrines that housed them, along with the priests and the priestesses who took care of the shrines. Worshippers brought offerings of meat (live animals), wine, fruit, vegetables and money. The caretakers of the shrines sold the food products, pocketed the money and thus earned a living and provided for the upkeep of the facility. It was big business and an established part of Athenian life.

We are somewhat acquainted with Greek and Roman gods and their mythology. This form of religion is described as polytheism — a belief in many gods. The Greek gods preceded the Roman versions, and often the

Romans simply Latinized the Greek gods. For example, the Greek god Hermes became the Roman god Mercury. Many gods were honoured in Athens at this time and their shrines lined the streets. Each shrine would contain an artistic representation of the god and usually an altar. Some shrines would probably remind us of a modern kiosk. They were not all grand monuments but each would be made out of stone, perhaps marble, or granite.

It is said of Paul that 'his spirit was provoked'. Most biblical commentators interpret this to mean that it upset Paul that the Athenians were so superstitious and immersed in idolatry. I have another idea. I cannot prove it, but it may be that Paul was reminded of his own religious experience. Paul's own rabbinical training had taken place in the school of Hillel, whose chief rabbi was Gamaliel. Paul was a scrupulous Pharisee. He kept the law thoroughly and later wrote of this time in his life that regarding the law he was blameless (Phil. 4:6). Paul had been very religious. He had meticulously kept the myriad of kosher laws, for instance, and followed their extensive restrictions.

At the same time, Paul had a heart hunger after God. He wanted to know the true and the living God. I think that as Paul wandered through Athens he thought, 'These Athenian people have a hunger to know and serve God, but all they actually have is superstition and idol worship.' Paul knew that mere religion and ritual were not going to get them anywhere. Theirs was what we refer to as 'works' religion. Through religious observance, the Athenians hoped their gods would be kind to them and prosper them. A great deal of Greek thought had to do with luck, fortune, avoiding evil and securing blessings. It was manipulation; it was essentially bargaining with the gods. It was trying to get whatever god it was to do something for you and to look with favour upon you. And if the issue had to do with life or death, you had better bring a big offering. If it were just a small thing, like having a good business trip, maybe a *denarius* (one day's wages) would do.

The Athenians were trapped in a magical world. That is what magic essentially is — an attempt to manipulate the gods. Magic does not necessarily have to involve a witch, a wizard or a sorcerer. It can simply be the attempt to get the gods to act in your favour by the performance of some kind of ritual.

I think that Paul sympathized with the Athenians; they reminded him of himself. Paul had been a seeker. Before his conversion, when he was persecuting Christians, Paul thought he was honouring God. Think of the young Islamic men who killed themselves while crashing commercial airliners into the World Trade Center in New York in 2001. They believed they were honouring their god and earning a place in paradise.

Paul realized that his earlier efforts had been absolutely fruitless. He was reminded, walking the streets of Athens, that he had been duped. He had never had any real peace or satisfaction during those days despite what his religious teachers said. He knew he had had no true relationship with God. His self-denying and strenuous efforts to please God had been wasted; therefore, his spirit was now stirred as he observed the hopeless efforts of the people of Athens.

This chapter is for people like Paul. It is for those who mistakenly believe that their religious observances are able to secure the favour, even the forgiveness, of God.

## Paul first preaches to the Jews

We know Paul's general missionary strategy: he would first preach to his kinsfolk, the Jews. As Luke records, 'So he argued in the synagogue with the Jews and the devout persons, and in the market place every day with those who chanced to be there' (Acts 17:17). As we read, there were also 'devout persons' attending the Jewish synagogues. These were Gentiles (non-Jews) who worshipped the God of Abraham, Isaac and Jacob. Judaism is monotheistic (a belief in one God), and some Gentiles, disgusted by the gross polytheism (a belief in many gods) of the Graeco-Roman world, were attracted to the God of Israel. Paul would speak to those in the synagogue first, but then he would go to the market place and present the message of Christ to Gentiles. By the way, this is the normal Christian thing to do — preach the gospel to the Jews first and then to the Gentiles (Rom. 1:16).

## The reaction of the philosophers

> Some also of the Epicurean and Stoic philosophers met him. And some said, 'What would this babbler say?' Others said, 'He seems to be a preacher of foreign divinities' — because he preached Jesus and the resurrection (Acts 17:18).

The Epicureans and the Stoics were two of the major philosophical schools extant in the first-century world. They called Paul a babbler. It was not a flattering term; it meant a loafer and a pseudo-intellectual. That was the way the elite Athenians described Paul. They did not understand Paul's message. It was probably the first time that they heard the Christian gospel and when Paul spoke of Jesus and the resurrection they thought he was talking about two different gods. The Greek word for resurrection is *anastasia*, a feminine word, and so they thought he was talking about Jesus and Anastasia.

## Seekers

And they took hold of him and brought him to the Areopagus, saying, 'May we know what this new teaching is which you present? For you bring some strange things to our ears; we wish to know therefore what these things mean' (Acts 17:19–20).

Paul was not being arrested; he was essentially invited for a more careful and reasoned presentation of his message. The Areopagus, or Mars Hill in Roman parlance, was an outdoor courtroom. Criminal and civil cases were brought there and the elders of the city gathered to try them. This was the format of their judicial system. This event in Acts probably did not occur on an ordinary court day but it was still the appropriate forum for such an examination.

I can imagine Paul walking to the Areopagus thinking: 'This is my opportunity. This is what I've been hoping for, to have a chance to present to the whole city of Athens, including the leading citizens, the story of Jesus.' I can imagine him praying, 'Lord, may your Holy Spirit help me to communicate with these seekers and do it in a way that would bring honour and glory to you.'

Paul was sensitive to the situation the Athenians were in. And I hope to be sensitive to the arguments and questions of seekers today. I remember that before I was converted, I had so many issues to raise — I wanted answers to serious questions and it was difficult to find someone who would talk about them with me. On the few occasions when I was able to engage Christians in conversation, they would sometimes become angry with me and we would end up in a dispute. These Christians would get angry with me because I was asking some pretty tough questions. They probably felt bad about it later and thought, 'Oh, this guy, Philpott, he will never become a Christian now, not after I've been arguing with him.' Nevertheless I did.

The call of God is powerful. Despite the ill treatment I received at the hands of some Christians I knew in the Air Force, God was able to overcome all that and I became a believer in Jesus.

God seeks us. God calls us. When we are called — and we are rarely able to identify this when it happens — we become seekers. I hope to be sensitive to that and bring the gospel to those who are also seekers.

## A national preoccupation

What about this Greek preoccupation with philosophy? Luke says, 'Now all the Athenians and the foreigners who lived there spent their time in nothing except telling or hearing something new' (Acts 17:21). Athens did not have the NFL, major league baseball, the NBA, hockey or soccer. There were the Olympic games and other games of the sort, but sports were not as pervasive as they are in our society. They did not have movies or television, though they did have plays and dramas — theatre was one of their main forms of entertainment. There were no radios, compact discs, DVDs, computers or cameras. It was not just a quick trip in the car over to the beach or to the mountains, either. You can imagine that to be able to have something of interest to discuss would be a major form of entertainment in Athenian culture.

## Very religious people

Earlier I mentioned that some of the Athenians might not have taken the gods and goddesses seriously. However, the gods were a prominent part of the religious fabric of the day. There were so many gods and goddesses in Athens that there must have been a lot of very religious people too.

The account in Acts continues: 'So Paul, standing in the middle of the Areopagus, said: "Men of Athens, I perceive that in every way you are very religious"' (Acts 17:22). Few today want to identify themselves as 'religious' — some because they are afraid of the connotations and others because they think they will be slotted into a certain category or idea of religion. I do not say I am religious, but I do say I am a Christian — a follower of Jesus.

I remember going through a period when I was superstitious. I had a lucky penny, which I inserted into a little tin horseshoe. I also carried a rabbit's foot in my pocket for a while. There were a number of quirky things I practised in my teenage years that were essentially superstitious in nature, and almost bordered on the religious. I know how attractive religion and ritual can be.

Although I generally have little interest in religious ritual, I have to admit that there is a part of me that is sometimes attracted to its ceremony. Years ago, on a bleak winter evening, I visited Canterbury Cathedral in England. What a place! I had read some fascinating stories associated with the cathedral, especially of Thomas à Becket and how some knights of King Henry killed that great saint. Being in that cavernous, incredible stone structure gave me a sense of awe. The light of flickering candles, the smell of incense, the rustle of clerical robes, the soft sound of footsteps reverberating off distant stone walls supported by flying buttresses, the music of the choir intoning a Gregorian chant — yes, there was an attraction.

## Worshipping an unknown god

For as I passed along, and observed the objects of your worship,
I found also an altar with this inscription, 'To an unknown god'
(Acts 17:23).

This is a real-life snapshot of Paul. While entering the city of Athens, he had found an altar with this unusual inscription, 'To an unknown god.' The Athenians were so scrupulous in their religious observance, and worried that they would slight one of the gods, that they erected an altar dedicated to an unknown god — just in case. And that is what religion can do to you. How quickly it can become obsessive or compulsive!

Religion can make a fanatic out of you. It can make you into an extremist because you feel that in order to win the favour of the god of your choice you have to be an incredibly obedient, devout person. But there is no end to it — no peace, no fulfilment, no assurance and no security.

The story comes to mind of Martin Luther, the Catholic priest who started the Protestant Reformation in Germany in the early sixteenth century. He was a monk in an Augustinian monastery, and in his devotion he would crawl over the rough stone steps of the monastery on his bare knees, even in the dead of winter. He bloodied his knees in order to show God his extreme devotion. Later when he came to know Christ, he saw that salvation was based on faith alone in Jesus and not on any religious work or activity that he could do. Luther's realization was the main catalyst of the Protestant Reformation. Some others also realized that the religion of the medieval Catholic Church was simply religion and that it had little to do with genuine, biblical Christianity. Luther and other Reformers like

John Calvin, Ulrich Zwingli, John Knox and the early Baptists saw that forgiveness could not be earned. No matter how devout, religious or sincere you are it does nothing but leave you empty. Perhaps it makes you proud and maybe deceived, but it does not bring you into a place of favour with God.

What kind of God would he be if he would reward those who are able to barter or bribe? Would this be a loving, merciful God? How about those who could not afford to do that? How much of a bribe would you have to pay? How many good deeds would you have to perform? If you had to say, 'Look, God, at what I did', would this be a God worthy of your love and devotion?

Understanding biblical Christianity is discovering you cannot buy God's acceptance or approval. No matter what you do, you cannot earn his favour; it is a matter of God loving us. God forgives our sins because he loves us in Christ. Eternal life is God's gift to us because he wants us to be in his presence in heaven for ever. Forgiveness and the gift of everlasting life come out of the desire, the will and the love of God alone.

## Doing good

Doing good is a part of the Christian life. We are called to this and God gives us the ability and the strength to do good things. But these actions do not bring us into favour with God. As a believer, I do what good works I can, but nothing I do will earn me God's acceptance.

Moreover, after I become a Christian, I cannot achieve a higher status with God by doing good works. The Scriptures portray good works as our 'reasonable service', or our duty. Our works are to flow naturally out of a desire to be obedient followers of Jesus.

## The Lord of heaven and earth

The God who made the world and everything in it, being Lord of heaven and earth, does not live in shrines made by man, nor is he served by human hands, as though he needed anything, since he himself gives to all men life and breath and everything. And he made from one every nation of men to live on all the face of the earth, having determined allotted periods and the boundaries of their habitation, that they should seek God, in the hope that they might feel after him and find him. Yet he is not far from each one of us (Acts 17:24–27).

Paul made a sharp distinction between the God and Father of our Lord Jesus Christ and every god or god-concept that the Athenians had. He presented one God rather than a pantheon of gods. He spoke of one God who is the Creator of all things. No doubt most of the polytheists were offended at that point. And when Paul went on to speak of a resurrected Jesus, the Jews and Gentile converts to Judaism were not pleased either.

In this passage, we find the reason why we have an interest in God at all — he made us so. A desire to seek and to know the Designer, the Programmer, is built into our very being. In a real sense, part of our humanity is to be religious. The trouble comes when we believe that our rituals, ceremonies, good works, even doctrinal beliefs, are enough to satisfy God and earn his praise.

The Creator God is not served by human hands. Paul rejected the idea of pleasing God by bringing offerings and sacrifices and he attacked the very foundation of the religious beliefs of the Athenians. What can man give to God that he has not already given to us?

Someone might protest: 'Come on, Paul, that was not a very strategic move to make. You ought to have established common ground with these people. You ought to have pointed out some of the positive aspects of their religious teaching.' Paul was not interested in that sort of compromise. He was not interested in being ecumenical. He was not pursuing a position on the board of directors of the local interfaith council. What he was interested in doing was reaching out to those who were seeking God, those who had a hunger to know and experience God. And why should he not aim at the heart of the matter? That is why Paul preached the God of the Bible, the only Lord of heaven and earth.

## The seeker

In verse 27, Paul says 'in the hope that they might feel after him and find him'. The word 'might' is not in the Greek text. It is an attempt to translate a conditional clause (an 'if' clause). This particular clause is called a fourth-class condition. Here is what Paul said literally: 'If people seek God they probably will not find him' (author's paraphrase). That is the nature of the fourth-class condition — it probably will not happen. That is why the last phrase of verse 27 begins with the word 'yet.' Paul says, 'Yet he is not far from each one of us.'

Paul's preaching was as close as these Athenians had ever come to knowing about God. In God's providence, he had brought to the very religious a preacher to proclaim the gospel of Jesus — the truth of who Jesus is and what he did on the cross. God the Father sent God the Son to be the perfect sacrifice for our sin, and on the basis of the sacrificial death of Jesus, secured forgiveness of our sin and the gift of eternal life. That is why we call it 'good news'. The gospel has to do with who Jesus is, his death, burial and resurrection. When that message is preached, God comes near. This is why the presentation of the gospel should be at the forefront of the ministry of the Christian church.

God is interested in the seeker. Over long centuries, many in Athens sought for God but they were looking in the wrong places. As Paul explained after he had seen their mythical gods — those enshrined along the avenues of the city — these gods merely lead those seekers astray. But the Creator God, the God and Father of our Lord Jesus Christ — those who seek *him* will find him.

## The end of the story

The last three verses of Acts 17 describe the result of Paul's ministry in Athens: 'Now when they heard of the resurrection of the dead, some mocked; but others said, "We will hear you again about this." So Paul went out from among them. But some men joined him and believed, among them Dionysius the Areopagite and a woman named Damaris and others with them' (Acts 17:32–34).

There will always be those who will trust in Jesus, but we know from the Scriptures, even from the mouth of Jesus (Matt. 7:13–14), that most will not. For the majority, religion itself is enough. Being religious does not require repentance; it does not require trusting in Jesus. It does not make any difference which god you worship, sincere religious devotion gives the impression that you are pleasing a deity and doing the right thing. And so, most people will settle for religion alone.

Some people will be dissatisfied with religion alone and some seekers will hear the message of Jesus and know it to be the truth. However imperfectly the gospel message may be presented, the Holy Spirit may call you to Jesus. Do not be deceived into thinking that being very religious will earn you points with God. Instead, be like Dionysius and Damaris who heard of the one true God, and his Son Jesus Christ, and believed.

# CHAPTER 11

# You have been duped if you think sin is inexpensive

S in is more expensive than you think — there are hidden costs. For those who recoil at the word 'sin' let me express my sincere apologies. Would it be better if I use 'transgression'? How about 'error'? Probably 'iniquity' would be no help at all. 'Character defect' is substituted for 'sin' in 12-step programmes (such as Alcoholics Anonymous). No matter how you choose to approach it, please understand that I use the short, bittersweet word 'sin' for no other reason than economy.

Have you ever thought, 'If I could have back all the money I have wasted, I would be a wealthy person'? I raise my hand. If I had all the money that I squandered doing the stupid things I have done, I might have accumulated a sizeable amount of money — and you probably would be a little farther along too. We all know our waywardness has cost us, if in nothing else than cold, hard cash. It is the hidden costs that are the trouble, however, because we do not have to settle these accounts until later. These costs can be put into four basic categories.

## Economic costs

The first category is economic — the money we actually lose. It may be gambling debts, a wrecked car, furniture destroyed in a rage, a crime committed when we were desperate, a divorce, a road-rage incident, court costs, lost jobs, missed opportunities — the list goes on. If we were sharing in a group right now, I imagine we would hear some interesting tales. Sin can be quantifiable; there have been definite losses.

Greed got its hold on me some years ago. I had a stockbroker's licence and I thought I was quite adept at trading stocks — actually a practice called day trading. At first, I did well. I made some decent money quite quickly. This proved to be my undoing. Thinking I was smarter than the rest, and fuelled by my greed, I managed to lose a sizeable amount of an inheritance my wife had received. The IRS knows exactly what my sin cost me. But this was cheap compared to what many have lost.

## Social costs

The second category is social because sin affects our associations, our relationships and our family life. I mentioned divorce under the first category because it can be expensive, but it also changes our personal world. Having been through a divorce, I know what I am talking about. After all these years, I am still paying a personal price.

Long-term friendships have fallen victim to sin. Strong ties, decades in the making, may be broken by our unrighteous behaviour. Shame and embarrassment may mean having to leave a home, a community or a job. Feuds, lawsuits or squabbles over an inheritance have costs that may be high in terms of actual dollars, but our social world can be drastically altered as well. The loss of community, associations and fellowship are a heavy price to pay.

## Psychological costs

The third category is psychological. Sin can pack a powerful emotional punch. Some people suffer great psychological trauma due to the sin in their lives and, of course, the sin in the lives of other people.

Volunteering at San Quentin Prison has taught me something about what psychologists call character disorders. In prison, there are many sociopaths and psychopaths. The consciences of these people do not function properly and they often view people merely as objects to fulfil their own needs or desires. These can be truly dangerous people. Over the years, sin piled upon sin tears down the proper functioning of the conscience and the psychological price is steep.

Many people are controlled by an anxiety or phobic fear. I have had more than one of these and know from first-hand experience how debilitating these can be. Psychologists may think I am on slippery ground when I suggest that sin has anything to do with anxiety, but when I look at my own sin, I can see a connection between that and my neurotic anxiety.

Once I experienced God's forgiveness of my sin, I finally began to experience a healthier emotional life.

Allow me to bring up the issue of homelessness. At Miller Avenue we host what we call the 'Saturday Lunch' for the homeless and for those whose budget does not meet all their grocery expenses. For years now I have mingled with the guests and have seen for myself their psychological deterioration, often as a result of alcohol and/or drug abuse. We can say, without being insensitive, that sin is at the bottom of most of it. Yes, the emotional cost of sin is astronomic. And, as civil servants who manage the public funds know, the price in terms of real dollars is also very high.

## Spiritual costs

The fourth category is spiritual. Sin affects us spiritually because it cuts us off from a relationship with God. Separated from God we are left without any sense of direction, to put it mildly. Our quest for wholeness and peace can be consuming, leading to many blind alleys and disappointments. Burdened with guilt and a sense of being unforgiven, we suffer emotionally and spiritually. Lacking self-esteem, because we are not living in fellowship with God, we may be driven to fruitless attempts to reach a sense of well-being. Living to satisfy ourselves (rather than honour and love God) and without ultimate meaning in our lives, we may end up cynical and jaded. And unforgiven sin must ultimately cost us the incalculable — *eternal* separation from the presence of God.

## Some 'deadly' sins

Let us consider the cost of some of the more common sins. I am not going to go into them extensively; I am merely going to describe them enough so you will be able to say, 'Oh yes, I know about that one.'

## Greed

Many of you followed the stories in the media about Enron, the American gas utility giant that imploded, damaging thousands of working people's lives. Many commentators concluded that the mammoth failure was caused by greed and arrogance. The insatiable desire for more will cost all of us a lot of money, but the greed on the part of the major players at Enron is going to cost them far more than they could imagine if they were to die without their sin being forgiven. There would be no choice except for the great Judge to exclude them from his presence. That is a nice way of saying that God would — he must actually — cast them into hell. That is a big price to pay for a few guilty dollars.

Have you considered the tremendous cost of gambling? The hooked and blinded gambler will brag about the $100 he or she won but will neglect to tell about the $1,000 lost. The paltry win is enough to send him or her back again and again to the tables, even when it seems insane to do so. And, oddly, many state governments and Indian tribes seem to think they are going to solve their economic problems by promoting the gambling industry. Essentially, they get people hooked on gambling (which some now call a disease and others call an addiction on the same level as alcohol and drug abuse) but never mind, we will get needed money for schools and other worthy institutions. Gambling may now be the 'number one' industry in America in terms of actual cash growth. The bottom line is greed.

Greed means that you never get enough and you never have enough. It produces driven, stressed-out individuals. Greed may lead to the Faustian-type sin where you sell your soul for a little bit more. We lose both our integrity and our hope. When we are driven by greed, we do not experience the peaceful enjoyment of the simple life and the pleasure all around us. The sin of greed is tremendously expensive.

## Sloth

The sin of sloth may not resonate with you right away. It is actually a sin I rarely mention. Do you know what sloth is? We might approach it by using a synonym like 'laziness'. I know about this one. Now you may not think that a 'Type A' person like myself would be tempted by sloth, but I am. I am not referring to sluggishness — the feeling that we need to take some time off and regroup. Sloth is giving up; it is expecting to be taken care of.

I am not simply espousing the Protestant/Puritan work ethic or making a hero out of the driven individual who does not know how to relax and enjoy life. It is common knowledge that both work and rest are normal aspects of life. Too much of either can tip the balance and some have lost the equilibrium completely and have given in to sloth. This sin has a powerfully depressing effect, often rendering people incapable of providing for themselves. Slothful people have given up. They are interested in protecting themselves, comforting themselves, pampering themselves, and will retreat into themselves and give up doing something, if there is not something easily and clearly in it for them.

I am glad to know that sloth is a sin because otherwise I would more readily give in to it. It would erode my self-confidence and affect my ability to perform altogether. The sin of sloth can be very costly.

## Sexual immorality

There is also the sin of sexual immorality. These costs are obvious: disease, broken relationships, loss of integrity, mistrust and incarceration, to name a few. Misuse of sex twists us and prevents us from having a normal, healthy sex life. Many lose their sexuality altogether by becoming obsessed with sex and pursuing it beyond all bounds. It costs many people their lives and because of the dramatic spread of HIV/AIDS, it may yet cost many more.

Sexual sin produces an unusually high degree of guilt and shame. This guilt is debilitating because the sinful person, weighed down by remorse and shame, will want to hide from God. I believe that God has hard-wired into us basic sensibilities about sex that are natural and normal. Through the revealed will of God in the Scriptures, we are explicitly acquainted with the rightness and wrongness of sexual expression. I wonder how few of us go unscathed when it comes to our sexuality. Many have twisted and warped what God intended to be a unique and beautiful union in marriage. Yet sexual unfaithfulness and deviation (meaning sex outside of the marriage bond) is one of the most potent means of driving people away from God. The result, if there is no turning to the Saviour for forgiveness, is eternal death. Sexual sin is costly indeed.

## Anger

The next sin is anger. Anger results in everything from domestic violence, to rape, pillaging, murder, racial and ethnic hatred, and much more. Everyone gets angry from time to time. Even Jesus showed anger, but the anger I have in mind, that I define as sinful, is that which grips the heart and mind and will not let go.

Volunteers at San Quentin Prison become aware of the trouble anger creates. I have personally observed, or sometimes just sensed, what I call a 'reservoir of anger' in many of the convicts. Most of the men have had problems growing up. They have experienced circumstances and events completely outside their control like physical and sexual abuse, poverty, early exposure to drugs, failure at school, absent parents (mostly fathers), failure on the playground or entrapment into a gang culture. During their critical formative years, a reservoir of anger developed inside them and they did not have the tools to empty it. As a result, it grew until the level rose above the dam and spilled out into some kind of horrible event. I am not being a 'bleeding heart liberal' either — this is simply how it is.

Some of the San Quentin inmates are physically or mentally handicapped and would never be able to make it in the real world. They may understand this too; they know how different they are and it makes them angry. Unless their anger is properly dealt with, it can lead to sin. The chances of dealing with their anger, or even recognizing their true condition, is remote at best. As a result there are rape, murder, drug addiction and senseless violence — all rising up out of this reservoir of anger.

Society holds individuals who act out of anger and hurt others accountable in order to protect itself. Collectively we cannot shrink from this unpleasant enterprise of locking up dangerous people. The cost for victims and criminals is monstrously high but the spiritual costs are far higher. A person does not have to land in prison to be guilty of the sin of anger. Jesus put it this way: 'I say to you that every one who is angry with his brother shall be liable to judgement; whoever insults his brother shall be liable to the council, and whoever says, "You fool!" shall be liable to the hell of fire' (Matt. 5:22). The only realistic conclusion must be that we are all guilty of the sin of anger.

## Substance abuse

'Drugs, sex, and rock and roll' is a phrase everyone knows, and it leads off with drugs. By substance abuse, I mean mostly drug and alcohol abuse, but there are many other types of substance abuse. You can probably recite a list as well as I can. Let me simply say that life is hard, harder for some than others, and substance abuse becomes a way out of the chaos and pain. However, being drunk or under the influence of drugs leads to more of a hell than the one the abuser is hoping to escape.

Of course, not all substance abusers are looking to escape the pain of living; some are trapped. Alcohol and drugs sneak up on them, little by little. Many do not fit the profile of the desperate drunk or drug addict, but are caught in the nightmare anyway. These people may never show up at a 12-step meeting, but they are candidates none the less. For these people it is a slow slide into hell, and the process of rationalizing their behaviour is simpler for them. The costs here are often hidden, due to the ability to maintain a semblance of normal life. But abusers are not at peace and will shy away from the message of the gospel because of their guilt and shame. The cost, finally, is beyond measure.

## Lying

Lying is probably the most universal of all sins. I have trouble with it myself. We protect and defend ourselves and often stretch the truth, even if only just a little bit.

Do you lie? How about paying your taxes? We hate the fact that the government gets so much of our money and then wastes it on over-priced hammers and other absurdities. We so easily justify cheating and lying and we become 'creative' with our tax forms.

In our personal relationships we have a hard time refraining from stretching the truth to protect our image or to enhance ourselves in the eyes of others. Reality is bent or twisted for self-serving purposes — but it is lying none the less. If we are caught in an embarrassing situation, we are known to slip and slide. Lying is ubiquitous.

Lying slowly tears away at our conscience. Lying, and not being caught at it, is terribly expensive. Some people are slick, smooth and clever and can look you right in the eye and tell downright lies. It is the liar who suffers the most, in terms of a healthy conscience. Over time, the liar moves closer and closer towards the boundaries of emotional health.

## Stealing

The *San Francisco Chronicle* ran a story about a social worker who was supposed to be distributing Christmas toys to kids who would not otherwise receive any. Unhappily, he stole the best gifts and gave them to family members and friends. He got caught and lost his job. I do not recall how many felonies he had committed nor how many years he would be locked up. There can be a high cost for stealing.

A character disorder, which is a loss of a properly functioning conscience, may begin with thievery. Young children steal. As a child, I would take dimes and quarters from off my father's dresser. He would put his change in a special copper bowl he had made in the Portland shipyards during World War II and I would steal from it. I got a few dollars but it had a bad effect on me. In my home, I have a small ceramic bowl that my kids made in an art class where I keep my spare change. I told my children that they could take any money they want from it because I did not want them stealing money and having a bad conscience about it.

When I was in the military, I was stunned at the extent of the thievery. My friends and I stole from our government. We had 'midnight chow' for the late shift at the hospital at Travis Air Force Base where I was a medic. The cars would be backed up to the mess hall's loading dock and whole sides of beef were carted away. I would laugh at it before I was a Christian. After I became a Christian, I understood that it was wrong.

As a lowly enlisted medic, I made very little money; in fact, I barely survived. I had a wife and two small children and every once in a while I would walk out with eggs, bread, butter, milk and the like. I reasoned, 'The government owes me.' That is always what the thief says, 'Well, they owe me.' You may think you are 'owed' something but that does not give you a licence to steal.

The sin of stealing has a major effect on the thief. After a while, his conscience does not function very effectively. (Probably the most vivid example I can think of is the fictional character Hannibal, played by Anthony Hopkins, in *The Silence of the Lambs*. The brilliant psychiatrist had a character disorder. He could commit the most horrible crimes without remorse.)

## Envy

Envy is the inability to be content with who we are and what we have. We want what someone else has, either in real life or in fiction, and so we are not content. We simply 'can't get no satisfaction' as the song goes. Envy may lead a person into adopting a victim mentality. It may lead to anger and hatred, thievery and lying, or worse.

In high school, I compared myself with others, especially other kids who played sports. I wanted to be a well-known and well-liked athlete, but I never achieved that status and I would envy those who did. Envy kept me from forming friendships, tended to make me feel like an outsider and, of course, it did not help my self-esteem. I started to see myself as less than okay; the envy even made me feel angry towards myself.

Envy is subtler than many sins. It lacks concrete expression, but is often behind some of the more blatant sins like lying and stealing. Envy has tremendous power to pervert and twist lives and relationships.

## Unbelief

Unbelief is the ultimate sin and easily the most dangerous of them all. It is unforgivable because it results in a rejection of Jesus.

All sin is forgivable; no one is beyond the long reach of God's powerful saving arm. God is indeed loving and merciful, not willing that we should suffer the consequences of our sin (2 Peter 3:9). His desire is that we be forgiven. But sinful behaviour may easily lead to the sin of unbelief. Why?

One answer is the fear of judgement. Deny the lawful existence of a judge, or reject law and order itself, and a temporary fix is the result. The extreme result of this position is anarchy or chaos, both of which have their advocates. Could atheists and agnostics be closet anarchists? Those who live outside the law usually despise authority and would do away with it if they could.

Unbelief is a common strategy for those who want to continue in their sinful ways. Guilt may be repressed temporarily, from the conscious mind anyway, but the all-knowing God is aware. Sin will not merely go away or be magically expunged from the books. No, it must be forgiven; it must be dealt with. This is what the life and work of Jesus were all about.

What a mess our sin can get us into! Sometimes our sins are deep, and interwoven and overlapping. Greed, envy or anger may be behind stealing, and lying, of course, goes along with it. There is often coveting too — a sin I am not going to get into here. Sexual sin is apt to lead us into many other sins to cover it up. Unbelief, the final refuge of the guilty sinner, only serves to provide temporary comfort. The point is that sin is like soup: everything gets thrown in, stirred around and assimilated. Sin makes life so complicated and crazy; it wears us out. It seems nearly impossible to break free of a sin-cycle and start over but, again, we are duped if we think there is no way out.

## The text: Romans 6:20–23

> When you were slaves of sin, you were free in regard to right-eousness. But then what return did you get from the things of which you are now ashamed? The end of those things is death. But now that you have been set free from sin and have become slaves of God, the return you get is sanctification and its end, eternal life. For the wages of sin is death, but the free gift of God is eternal life in Christ Jesus our Lord (Rom. 6:20–23).

'When you were slaves of sin...' Paul writes. Sin is that way. It makes a slave of us; it owns us. The key word is slave or *dulos* in Greek. It means bond slave; the bond slave is owned. So, outside of Christ, we are slaves of sin. The return or wages for our sin is nothing less than spiritual death. Spiritual death is eternal separation from God — the greatest possible cost.

Being a slave to sin is different from being a slave to righteousness. Righteousness is peace with God. The wages of righteousness is eternal life. When you are a slave to sin you are owned by sin. You are not owned by righteousness but free from righteousness. 'Free' is a relative term in this context. Freedom to sin is a strange way to talk; it is freedom though, much like the freedom to slowly poison oneself.

In verse 21 Paul writes, 'But then what return did you get from the things of which you are now ashamed?' In other words, Paul is asking: 'What good came of sin? What did you earn from it? What did you reap? What was the fruit of your sin?' Shame is the answer. All that is accrued to you after years of investing in sin is shame.

The mention of shame might cause one to wonder, 'What shame do I have?' Consider this: You are standing before a holy and righteous God, the Creator of all that exists, naked and with nothing but your sin. Even the most conscience-seared psychopath will be shamed.

How expensive sin is! Our sins cost us economically, socially and psychologically; but sin costs us spiritually, and that is the biggest cost: 'The end of those things is death.'

'But now that you have been set free from sin...' (Rom. 6:22). Notice Paul's wording: 'been set free'. The word 'been' indicates the passive voice. It does not mean 'now that you have freed yourself' or 'now that you are free'. Paul's meaning is, 'You have *been* freed, you have *been set* free.' The problem with sin is that you cannot do anything about it yourself. You are trapped. The slave must be set free.

Freedom from the high cost of sin is the work of God alone. Our sin places us in a situation where we are completely powerless. We are stuck. We owe a debt we cannot pay. Do you see it? We have no resources to rely upon; no credit or loan is forthcoming. Now we see the glory of the gospel — we have been set free from sin. The passive voice indicates that someone did something for us. Paul writes that we have been '... set free from sin and have become slaves of God.' Now we belong to him. It is a transfer of ownership.

The last part of verse 22 explains that 'the return you get is sanctification and its end, eternal life'. The difference is huge. Can you imagine a greater contrast in wages? On the one hand sin brings certain and eternal death; but on the other hand we have sanctification — being owned or set aside for God — and eternal life. Eternal life versus eternal death — an infinite, qualitative distinction of the highest order. As bond slaves to sin we do not realize the tremendous price we have been paying and the tremendous price that yet remains to be paid.

In the following verse, Paul sums it up: 'For the wages of sin is death' (Rom. 6:23). There it is. We see only the problems our sin creates for us, but we really do not see the full cost. Paul, however, had the courage to clearly lay out the truth about the matter. The wages of sin is *death*.

'But the free gift of God is eternal life.' The word *charisma*, 'gift' in the text, can be rendered 'grace'. A gift or grace cannot be earned, only received, and that is why 'free' is added to the English translation so that the reader will understand that Paul means eternal life is a gift. There is a tremendous contrast between wages and a gift.

Someone might protest, 'I do not have very many sins. I probably do not owe that much.' In case there happens to be someone so very naïve about sin, I want to be clear that one sin is enough. One sin or many — the wage is still death. We have a way of comparing ourselves to other people. 'Oh, I do not have very much in the old sin account. I have been pretty good,' we think. How dangerous that thinking is! One sin is enough.

The gospel is two-sided. It starts out with the law — 'the wages of sin is death' — but it ends with 'the free gift of God is eternal life in Christ Jesus our Lord'. You have earned death. You will receive the wages of your sin. It is absolutely inescapable. If you think anything other than that, it is only the measure of how much you have been duped and deceived.

The good news is that Jesus paid the price for our sins. That is what he did on the cross. Consider again the situation. We are powerless but Jesus did what we could not. He has already taken our death upon himself. While on the cross, God the Father placed our sin upon God the Son, Jesus. The God-man, Jesus the Messiah, the perfect sacrifice for sin, died in our place. His blood was shed, the cleansing blood of the Lamb, and it covered our sin.

How slaves of righteousness love to hear the gospel preached! We see our unworthiness, we see the awful nature of our own sin and the shame of it comes up before us, but how pleased we are to see that Jesus paid the whole price! He took our sin upon himself and his great delight is to give us the free gift of eternal life. What a glorious message we have! It starts out being very awful. It ends up being very wonderful.

# CHAPTER 12

# You have been duped if you think that the Bible is not trustworthy

I t is unwise, even dangerous, to ignore the Bible. Jesus said, 'Heaven and earth will pass away, but my words will not pass away' (Luke 21:33). Men and women, however, do ignore the Bible. Perhaps it is because of various myths that have circulated about it — myths such as: 'It is written by men', 'It is full of errors', 'It was changed by the church', 'It is hard to understand', or 'You can make it say whatever you want it to.'

I first tried reading the Bible when I was twenty years old. I got halfway through the first chapter of Genesis before I gave up. A week or so later I tried again and finished the whole first chapter. Then I gave up again. It made no sense to me. I wondered what was so special about the Bible anyway. No doubt there are others like me. Let me make this simple appeal: do not give up on the Bible.

## The reason for the chapter

In this book, I am constantly appealing to the Bible as my authority, my primary source, all the while knowing that the Christian Scriptures are problematic to non-Christians. How then can I proceed? I could rely on my experience over against the Bible. But why take my word for anything, especially for something as important as truth and eternal life?

The Christian apologist must deal with these limitations. We are not dealing with mathematics or science — we are engaged in the realm of the spirit, which is not amenable to the scientific process of testing and verification. Therefore, I have a sense of frustration. I trust the Bible, I am hoping to win a fair hearing for it, but at the same time, I cannot prove its reliability. Like every Christian witness before me, I must rely on the ministry of the Holy Spirit. That may sound strange to some, but that is how it works. The Christian makes his or her case in the best possible manner, but must then depend on the Holy Spirit of God to apply his truth.

I want to explain to you now why I, and millions of other Christians, hold the Bible in such high esteem. I also want to address the following paradox: many of us who now love the Bible once despised and even hated it. It would not be exaggerating to say that some of us actually feared it. We did not doubt it unconsciously. We were purposely ignoring the most loved and read book the world has ever known. How could this be?

## Why a Bible?

If there were no Bible, would there be Christianity at all? No, because the Bible is the revelation of who God is and his purposes in Christ and in the world.

The ministry of Jesus, the 'days of his flesh', was confined to a particular time and space. An oral transmission of the message did in fact serve the first few generations after Jesus, and that might have sufficed to some degree for a longer period but, given the wide diversity of people and the multiplicity of cultures, languages and politics, an oral communication alone would have been limited. A pre-technological world, I mean a world without instant information through radio, television and the computer, demanded a form of communication better suited to the complexity of the situation. It required ink on paper, words bound and storable, economic and efficient — a book is the obvious medium to communicate the message to the widest possible audience.

## An accusation

Some say, 'You Christians think too highly of the Bible.' Non-Christians can be tempted to think like this because the Bible reveals some very difficult things that, if true, mean they are in big trouble. The Bible's judgement of sin and sinners is well known. I understand that argument, particularly from non-Christians.

There are some *within* the Christian tradition who say the same thing. They are found at the liberal end of the Christian spectrum and often join in the chorus: 'You fanatical Bible-thumpers are taking the Bible too seriously.' Most of the time I simply think to myself, 'I wish I were taking it *more* seriously than I am.' Sometimes I think, 'I wish you loved the book more than you do.'

A Christian publication that carried dozens of advertisements for Christian colleges and seminaries illustrates this point. Some of the institutions who advertised in the magazine were at the liberal end of the spectrum and I was struck that they made little or no reference to the Bible. In the advertisements for the more conservative schools, it was the opposite. These schools wanted prospective students to know, 'Come to our school: we teach the Bible.' The liberal schools, on the other hand, usually emphasized a warm and fuzzy, therapeutically-oriented curriculum. My point is: not all people in the 'Christian' camp have a high view of the Bible.

## The usual approach

I enjoy debating with people who do not give the Bible much credence. But it is frustrating to talk with people who have a high view of the Bible yet feel that all that is necessary to defend the Bible is to quote 2 Timothy 3:16, 'All scripture is inspired by God', or 2 Peter 1:20–21: 'First of all you must understand this, that no prophecy of scripture is a matter of one's own interpretation, because no prophecy ever came by the impulse of man, but men moved by the Holy Spirit spoke from God.' Christians quote these verses and think they have settled the issue. I know this from firsthand experience: I used the same approach. It did not dawn on me that I was using the document to prove the authenticity of the document. As a result, people who were looking for answers became irritated with me. At the time, I did not understand their frustration, but now I realize that there is something lacking in just quoting these passages.

## A circular argument

The Bible contains statements that claim divine inspiration for itself. For example, the New Testament writers, quoted above, affirm the inspiration of the Old Testament. Thus, Bible verses are quoted in an attempt to prove the Bible is truth based on what the Bible itself says. This is what may be called a circular argument.

As I have stated, I have used the argument myself. But many do reason, 'Wait a minute, you cannot use the document to prove the validity of the document. Slap some pages in between black leather and print "Holy Bible" in gold letters on it and, "Voilà!" There must be more to it than that; there must be some external or forensic evidence.'

In the Christian community, there have been significant apologists who have argued for the authenticity of the Scripture. Josh McDowell and

F. F. Bruce, among many others, have done excellent work in this area. But sometimes Christians are made to feel like liberals if they should even begin to address the issue. I have to take the risk of dealing with this because my interest is not in pleasing the Christian community, either left or right. My concern is for those who have dismissed the Bible altogether. I want to be able to show you, or at least make a good case, that you have been deceived if you dismiss the witness of the Bible.

## The Scripture is self-validating

New Testament writers do validate the authority and inspiration of the Hebrew Scriptures and no one more so than Jesus himself. This is as we would expect. There is a sense, then, that my point about the use of a circular argument to prove the authenticity of the Bible is wrong. My view is that God did inspire the Bible, a point I will expand on later. At the same time I know, from considerable personal experience as a pastor, that Christian efforts to promote the authority of the Bible fall flat, particularly when the Bible itself is appealed to as the primary evidence. To simply acknowledge the problem, I believe, is a step towards getting past it.

## My own view of the Bible

I completely accept Paul's and Peter's defence of the Scriptures. I believe in the total inspiration of the Bible, and I mean the entire Bible: all of the words in all of the verses in all of the chapters in all of the books. I believe in the inspiration of the Word of God. I take the Bible seriously, since I believe it is directly from the Creator God. The Bible has many forms of literature — narrative, poetry, history, Gospels, letters and more — and these will be variously understood. It is not a simple task to know when to take things literally or figuratively. Christians disagree on matters of interpretation.

The 'Scripture' to which Paul and Peter referred to in the verses we quoted earlier is the Old Testament, the Hebrew Scriptures. The authors of books in the Old and New Testament probably had little or no idea that what they were writing was going to be looked upon as inspired by future generations. They did speak in the name of the Lord: Moses did and prophets like Jeremiah and Isaiah did. Still, the record of their words, collected into a document, does not carry the absolute proof to everyone that the result is the infallible Word of God. It is a matter of faith; it is a matter of revelation. And the unbeliever cannot be sure. If we are honest, even the believer struggles with it at times.

There was a time in my life, the summer between my first and second years in seminary, when I began to question the Bible. I had come from a conservative church that held to a very high view of Scripture. It seemed to me that my seminary professors held to a lesser view. (I have since realized that my perception was incorrect; they merely hoped I would examine the reason for my faith more closely.) More than once, my professors raised points that forced me to rethink my position about the Bible. For example, for the first time I realized that the Gospel writers, especially Matthew, Mark and Luke, differed over details. I did not understand the nature of a 'Gospel' book and, as a result, my faith was tested. I knew that if the Bible could not be trusted, then what could I trust? So much depended on what the Bible said. Here I was, a young man heading into pastoral ministry, and the foundation of my faith appeared to be fragile.

That summer proved to be a very trying time for me. What if the Bible was not reliable? What then was true? Did Jesus really die on the cross? Was he resurrected? Is he coming back?

Nothing miraculous occurred. The Bible remained a mystery to me. Yet, I found my solid ground to be Jesus himself. The new birth, or conversion, is a real thing. It happened to me and I knew Jesus was my Lord and Saviour — that much was settled. The Bible told me about Jesus, and is, of course, the primary source for knowledge of who Jesus is and what he did. I would stick with the Bible. I would preach it; I would teach it; I would trust it.

## Other 'scriptures'

Have you compared the Bible with other 'sacred' literature? If you have, you will see that the Bible reads completely different from them. Many have claimed supernatural inspiration for different books: the Book of Mormon, the Qur'an, The Course in Miracles and the Urantia Book. There is a long list of other books like these that claim to be inspired by somebody or something — usually by some god or angel. How can these books be evaluated? Some say these documents have similar ideas and should be treated on an equal plane with the Bible. It is a poor counterfeiter, however, who cannot produce a bill that will at least pass a cursory examination. There is usually some truth in whatever the document, some spiritual insight, something that will resonate with someone. Yet these other books tend to be self-consciously 'religious' and sound as if their writers want very much to seem holy and wise. But when you read the Bible, it does not read like these other books.

## Jesus and the Bible

Jesus quoted often from the Old Testament. He quoted from all five books of the Law of Moses: Genesis, Exodus, Leviticus, Numbers and Deuteronomy. He quoted from the Psalms and many of the Prophets. He knew the Scriptures well; he had a high view of them.

Many passages in the New Testament would serve to illustrate this, but let us consider Mark 7:9–13:

> And he said to them [the religious leaders], 'You have a fine way of rejecting the commandment of God, in order to keep your tradition! For Moses said, "Honour your father and your mother"; and, "He who speaks evil of father or mother, let him surely die"; but you say, If a man tells his father or his mother, 'What you would have gained from me is Corban' (that is, given to God)— then you no longer permit him to do anything for his father or mother, thus making void the word of God through your tradition which you hand on.'

Jesus clearly referred to the Hebrew Bible, and specifically to the Law of Moses, as the Word of God. This is very important to me since so much of my view of the Bible, as you already know, rests upon Jesus. Jesus also said, 'scripture cannot be broken' (John 10:35).

## A model

I am going to use a model to help us better understand that the Bible can be trusted as the inspired Word of God. It focuses on the consistency of three witnesses — three witnesses telling the same story and containing the same truth or point of doctrine. The three witnesses are these: the Old Testament, the Gospels and the writings of the early church. By early church, I mean the book of Acts, and those books or letters in the New Testament written by Paul, Peter, John, James and Jude.

What do I mean by 'consistency of witnesses'? Simply this: there is no doctrine believed by the early church that does not have its source in the teachings or actions of Jesus as recorded in the Gospels, and we do not see anything in the Gospels that we do not see, at least in seed form, in the Old Testament. It is the consistency of storyline and points of doctrine that matter.

All three witnesses — the Old Testament, the Gospels and the early church — are quite distinct from one another. They are written in two languages, with some Aramaic amongst Old Testament prophets, and are from at least two differing cultures, Hebrew and Græco-Roman. They were written over a period of fifteen centuries, yet their agreement in theme and theology is strong evidence for the inspiration of Scripture.

We will now consider several major doctrines that are consistent in all three witnesses. This topic is enormous and could be pursued by anyone with a Bible and a Bible concordance.

## The sovereignty of God

One of the most striking points of consistency has to do with the doctrine of the sovereignty of God. By this I mean that God acts as he wills — *he* chooses, *he* decides. In the book of Genesis, we have the account of God creating Adam and Eve, as well as the whole universe. This Creator God acted according to his own purpose and design. We observe his choice of Abel over Cain, Isaac over Ishmael, Jacob over Esau, and then his choice of Israel over all the other nations. God always acts in accordance with his holy nature and cannot be manipulated in any way.

In the Gospels, Jesus pointed out that we did not choose him but that he chose us (John 15:16). He also stated that no one could believe in him unless the Father made it possible. This is God's sovereignty — God takes the initiative.

As we come to Paul's letters, the doctrine of election, or God's choosing and predestinating, is a familiar theme (Eph. 1:3–6; Rom. 9). Since people have no ability at all to please God or forgive their own sin, it is an act of mercy or grace that a person is cleansed of sin. This again is God's sovereignty.

## The nature of God

A second point of doctrine has to do with the nature of God. We call these his attributes, among which are his holiness and righteousness. The revelation of these attributes is the same in the Old Testament, the Gospels and in the witness of the early church. God's attributes are the same whether the literary style is history, poetry, parable, preaching or teaching. The Bible is the story of God, regardless of who wrote each section. Jesus does not innovate on any point concerning the nature of God. Paul, Peter, John and the others all present the same facts as to the nature of God.

'Holy, holy, holy is the Lord of hosts', we read in Isaiah 6:3. The Old Testament prophet sounds the theme for the Holy One of Israel. God is separate from sin; he is righteous by nature. In the New Testament, part of the model prayer Jesus taught his disciples says, 'Hallowed be thy name' (Matt. 6:9). 'Hallowed' has to do with holiness. Writing to Christian churches, Peter said, 'he who called you is holy' (1 Peter 1:15). All three witnesses are perfectly consistent.

## Human nature

Another consistent doctrine concerns the nature of men and women. Created in the image of God, though creatures of flesh and blood, humans are held responsible by God to obey him — yet we rebel. In the Old Testament, Adam and Eve eat of the forbidden fruit. Then Cain kills Abel; later the prophets are rejected and stoned to death; and then God's own chosen people, the Jews, harden their hearts towards him. The theme of rebellion runs throughout the Old Testament.

We certainly see that Jesus knew what was in humans. This was the primary reason for the incarnation (Jesus becoming a man). Jesus came to earth to die in order to deal with sinful human rebellion. The Old Testament prophets said that the Messiah would die for the sin of the people (Isa. 53) and the Gospels tell the story of the cross. Jesus' death was purposeful and deliberate, the unfolding of the plan of a sovereign God. The early church proclaimed the necessity for sinful people to turn from their sin: 'All have sinned', said Paul (Rom. 3:23).

## The primary message of the Bible

We find the story of redemption, reconciliation and forgiveness in the Old Testament, in the preaching of Jesus and in the witness of the early church. Redemption means the paying of a price. Reconciliation means reuniting. Forgiveness means covering of sin.

These themes are portrayed repeatedly in the Old Testament, particularly in Genesis, and are the central theme of the life and ministry of Jesus. Jesus' life was the price that redeemed us from eternal death. Jesus, as mediator (he stands between us and the Father), by his death and perfect sacrifice, reconciles us with God. The death of Jesus, in which he takes our sin upon himself, satisfies the just demands of the Father so that our sin and rebellion may be forgiven.

The story of redemption, reconciliation and forgiveness are essentially on every page of the Hebrew Scriptures; they are the central story of the Gospels and they are the main preaching and teaching points of the early church. Indeed, the history of the early church is one of mission and evangelism; the message of Jesus is spread throughout the world. The gospel is for everyone because *all people* have sinned. Thus the gospel is global in nature. John writes, 'For God so loved the world that he gave his only Son, that whoever believes in him should not perish but have eternal life' (John 3:16).

## The model story

Consider the parable of the prodigal son found in Luke 15. It is a parable that Jesus told to his disciples, and to a larger crowd that included various Jewish religious leaders.

In this parable, Jesus speaks of a man who had two sons. The younger son announced to his father, 'I want my inheritance now.' He was too impatient to wait for his father to die; he wanted his inheritance right away. There was greed in his heart — it is the story of the human condition. His father let him exercise his free will, though he knew it would only bring disaster upon his precious offspring. He gave him his inheritance.

God had told Adam (and I summarize): 'Do not eat of that tree. For the day in which you do, you will surely die' (Gen. 2:16–17). God did not prevent Adam and Eve from eating the fruit. He did not put a barrier around the tree. They had the capacity to rebel against him. What Adam and Eve did, the prodigal did. That is *our* story as well — we are that prodigal, that son or daughter of the Father.

The young man took his inheritance, went into a far country, and did miserably with it. He did everything he had been taught not to do. He was finally reduced to the status of a slave, doing the most despicable work imaginable for a young Jewish boy — tending the swine. But he came to himself, an expression of repentance, and realized that he had sinned against God in heaven, as well as against his earthly father. He began the long trek home.

## Repentance

The theme of repentance is found throughout the Scripture. John the Baptist began his ministry with, 'Repent!' Jesus began his ministry with, 'Repent!' He said, 'Repent, for the kingdom of heaven is at hand' (Matt. 4:17).

The prodigal son repented; he went back home. The father, waiting and watching for him, saw him a long way off and ran to welcome and embrace the son that had been considered lost. There was a great celebration and the lost, 'dead' son was restored to his previous status.

This theme is the storyline of the Bible. It is the storyline of the Old Testament. It is the message of Jesus. It is a primary focus of the preaching of the early church.

There is yet another aspect to the story. Remember, there were two sons. The eldest son stayed home and did the right thing. He patiently worked and waited, figuring that his father would reward him at some point. The eldest son did not rejoice when his younger brother returned home; instead he whined to his father about the apparent favouritism. The older son could not grasp grace and mercy; he wanted the younger brother to have to pay the penalty for being a greedy rebel. This element of the story is also the theme of our humanness — we prefer the model of reward and punishment to grace. The prodigal son received grace from his father. This is foreign, even hateful, to a performance-based man or woman. Grace, God's acting for our good when he has every right to make us pay the ultimate price, is the story of the *love of God*. He does not give us what we deserve; he gives us what we cannot earn — forgiveness and love. This is the greatest story ever told.

## No conspiracy

Some people believe the Bible is the product of a conspiracy. I do not know how they can come to this conclusion except that they accept, uncritically, myths about the Bible such as, 'There was a conspiratorial church council that put the Bible together.' This, by the way, is one of the themes of *The Da Vinci Code*, a fictional novel by Dan Brown. Brown is depending on the ignorance of his readers, assuming that they will simply accept his view and not bother to 'look it up'. This is straightforward historical ignorance. 'Ignorance' is not a blaming word. It means 'without knowledge'. Few people know how the Bible actually came together.

I need not repeat the time, cultural and language factors that influenced the formation of the Old and New Testaments, but these are significant. The historical evidence reveals that the Holy Spirit orchestrated the whole process. Over long centuries, both the Old and New Testament books were collected together because of their authorship and their usefulness to the community of faith. Many questionable and spurious documents were rejected through an informal process, in churches scattered throughout Europe, North Africa, the Middle East and beyond. No committee or grand council selected the books to be included. By the time a fourth-century council did make a list of the authoritative books of the New Testament, the list had already been long established by the Christian community itself.

Let me reiterate. No one said, 'We are going to publish a sacred document.' No individual or group decided to put it all together, bind it in black leather, put 'Bible' on the cover and demand that everybody believe it. That is not how it worked. If you think otherwise, let me suggest two things. First, look it up. The history is there for all to read. Second, you have been deceived if you think the Bible is the result of some Christian conspiracy.

I would be suspicious of any other method of the development of the Bible. If claims were made for the Bible that it was channelled directly from Moses, the archangels Gabriel or Michael, or any other angel, spiritual master, spirit guide, even a being who identified himself as Jesus, as in the Course in Miracles, I would be on my guard. There was no financial motive involved in the production of the Bible. 'Follow the money trail' is a useful admonition, but there is no 'money trail' when it comes to the Bible. Who profited? Though books circulated — and this is true for both the Old and New Testaments — no author, publisher, printer or binder were putting together contracts, with royalties assigned and discount prices settled on. There was no organization, such as that which developed after the fourth century, controlling the whole of the church. We know of the denominations and large branches of Christendom today, but this is a very different reality from the early centuries of the church when the Bible came into being.

## Missing books

We sometimes hear of the 'lost books of the Bible'. The assertion is that books that should have been included in the Bible were left out because the 'church' did not like them, or their doctrines, such as reincarnation. This is also a theme in The Da Vinci Code.

Again, I must counter with, 'Look it up.' It did not happen. The early church — mostly the second and third-century church — rejected books that were written by Gnostics for example, who gave their documents titles like The Gospel of Peter, The Gospel of the Hebrews, The Gospel of Mary, and so on. These writers claimed that apostles or other New Testament figures wrote their books even though everyone knew they did not. The term pseudepigrapha (false writing) describes these books. The clamour over the 'lost books' of the Bible is erroneous and a waste of energy.

## Preservation of the Bible

God preserved the Scriptures over centuries. It is a thrilling story. If you consider the Old Testament, how many tried to destroy the scrolls! It is interesting to note that when the Dead Sea Scrolls were discovered (1947–1956), people thought, 'Now we are really going to find out about the Bible. We are going to discover that the Old Testament is a mess.' However, the Old Testament as we have it today turned out to be a reliable document, unchanged over the millenniums. In fact, there is not another document from antiquity that can even approach it for accuracy and internal integrity. Archaeology consistently supports the authority of Scripture. Some of the most dedicated archaeologists are those who hope to dis-prove the Bible. They have a hard time doing so: everything they find tends to validate the Bible. It is even more so with the New Testament. The thousands of documents we have of the New Testament books, some going back to the second century, provide abundant evidence to ascertain what the originals looked like before changes, edits and additions were made or crept into the New Testament documents. Yes, scribes made changes (purposely or inadvertently) and we know what these were. Again, you can look it up. Most of the newer translations indicate any passages where there are minor variations in the text of different ancient manuscripts and none of these affects any major point of doctrine.

How the Bible survived deliberate and determined attempts to destroy it is a remarkable story. How the Bible survived neglect, distortion and corruption — this again is an amazing story. The long and short of it is: God preserved his Word.

In addition, the Scripture is transcultural; it can be effectively translated into any language. If a language is complex like Chinese, English or Japanese, that is no barrier. If a language has a vocabulary of only 500 words, it is no obstacle at all. It does not matter what the culture, the race or the language is, the Bible is as reliable as it has ever been.

## The style of the Bible

I am impressed with the Bible for other reasons. One reason is its lack of fluffy religious language — that sticky sweet, syrupy language. It is not a flattering document and does not contain spiritual 'psychobabble'. It is not so esoteric that it is not applicable to everyday life; even children can read and understand it.

The Bible, on the other hand, is also full of paradoxes. There is the paradox of death and resurrection. The advertising people would complain: 'You have an executed criminal, a young Jewish man claiming to be God, who seems to be resurrected from the dead, and will return to judge the world at the end of history. You will have to do better than that.'

As a publisher, I would not have permitted such a document to be printed. Any publisher would have concluded, 'This isn't going to work. You need warm, fluffy, cosy stuff. The judgement themes and the scary material will not sell. And the main character, a God-man — nobody is going to believe that. And the double-talk about salvation: God electing and, at the same time, our needing to repent and believe. This is too complicated: make it simple. Get rid of the paradoxes. Get rid of the human writers with their sinful ways and inconsistencies, men like Paul and Peter. We need pristine spirits and lofty saints if we are going to call it the inspired Word of God. Let's clean this up or it will never sell.'

## A strong message

Many have a difficult time with the Bible because they do not like what it says about them. I hear of non-Christians who insist they like to read the Bible — I do not know what portion they have been reading, but they have not read the good parts yet. Once they do, they will have a different sense of it. I remember my attitude; I did not like it at all. It did not make any sense to me. But, as soon as I was converted, I loved it. You can always spot Christians — they love the Bible. They do not necessarily read it four or five hours a day, but they treasure the Bible. When Christians get together, they enjoy talking about what they have discovered in its pages.

Because of the blunt message of the Bible, there will always be detractors. All of us have sinned against a righteous and holy God and unless we turn from our sin, we are in the worst possible trouble — hardly an attractive message.

Let me be clear. I accept the Bible as the plain, straightforward Word of God. There are two ways that I accept the Scripture as the Word of God: subjectively, as it speaks to me, and objectively, that whether I believe in the Bible or not, it still is the Word of God. I do not have to believe in it to make it the Word of God — that is the subjective view. The Bible stands as the truth of God whatever my view of it — this is the objective view.

## One last big point

If I had to pick one reason why I believe that the Bible, from Genesis to Revelation, is the inspired and only Word of God, it would be because of Jesus. Jesus believed that the Hebrew Scriptures were inspired by God. He called the God who inspired the Old Testament his Father. He said, 'I do not say anything but what the Father has shown me and given me to say.' Jesus has ultimate integrity for me. I find nothing false in him: no pride, no arrogance and no sin. I rest my case on the person of Jesus himself. People have looked long and hard for psychological disturbance in him. It is not there. Over the centuries, critics have fine-sifted him, looking for the slightest taint of mental imbalance, and cannot find it.

The apostolic letters of the New Testament accurately reflect the teachings of Jesus. The documents that emerged in that primitive church, from the Gospels, through the letters, to the Revelation of John, are consistent with the message of Jesus and the natural culmination of the Old Testament.

## Do not take my word for it

I do not believe the Bible is the inspired Word of God because someone told me I ought to. I do not care about being approved and accepted by the Christian community. I am not going to base my life and death on some old book unless I am personally convinced that it is the truth. If my church, and every preacher in town, rejects me, I will not get on board to avoid their displeasure. Be sure about the Bible. When you are converted, you will become convinced. It will naturally arise; you will not have to talk yourself into it. The key is Jesus. Seek him. Follow him, and he will make it plain to you.

## A summary

We embrace these three witnesses — the Old Testament, the Gospels and the early church — and preach and teach from them. God has to do the rest. We simply bring the witness. In this short chapter, I do not expect to convince anyone that the Bible is the Word of God. Ultimately, I know it has to be the work of the Holy Spirit. But you have been duped if you can so easily dismiss the witness of the Bible. Jesus said, 'Heaven and earth will pass away, but my words will not pass away' (Luke 21:33).

# CHAPTER 13

# You have been duped if you think God is merely a 'higher power' or you settle for a God you can understand

This chapter is for my friends in 12-step rehabilitation programmes. I am hoping to build a bridge for those who have come to a place where they acknowledge a 'higher power'. My main point is this: God is more than a higher power.

Let us begin with Romans 15:5–6: 'May the God of steadfastness and encouragement grant you to live in such harmony with one another, in accord with Christ Jesus, that together you may with one voice glorify the God and Father of our Lord Jesus Christ.'

It is critical we see that God is both *God* and *Father* of our Lord Jesus Christ. The Creator God, the only God there is, is indivisibly connected to, or related to, Jesus the Messiah. This Jesus is Lord, meaning Lord or Master, of all there is.

Certainly, we recognize the limits of language and consequently must not directly or literally apply our human concepts of father and son to the Deity. Yet, we need to understand the unique relationship between God the Father and God the Son. To miss this is to misunderstand the very nature of God. Therefore, to see God as simply a higher power, unrelated and unconnected to Jesus Christ, is a mistake.

No other major spiritual figure claimed to be God 'in the flesh'. This claim is unique. Jesus consistently subordinated himself to the Father, all the while doing that which Deity alone could do. Jesus also prayed to the Father — which seems contradictory. This reveals something of the mystery of the Trinity, the three in one or the one in three. Jesus, God the Son, emptied himself (Phil. 2:5–8) and took on human flesh. He was perfectly obedient to the Father, which means, among other things, that he was without sin. Christians have attempted to describe the God-man nature of Jesus, to put into words what the Bible conveys about who Jesus is, and these attempts seem inadequate. Still, the Bible's presentation of the nature of Jesus demands the conclusion that God become man in Christ. This is logical in that the perfect sacrifice for sin must be both God and man. God to atone for sin, and man to actually die.

The second passage to consider is John 8:42: 'Jesus said to them, "If God were your Father, you would love me, for I proceeded and came forth from God; I came not of my own accord, but he sent me."'

Jesus was engaged in a dialogue with Jewish leaders who claimed to have a special relationship with God. Despite their appeals to orthodoxy, they were steadfastly rejecting Jesus. This was wrong because Jesus perfectly fulfilled all the prophecies about the coming Messiah. He also healed, cast out demons and did signs and miracles that attested to who he truly was. Also, he clearly and directly stated that God was his Father, thus claiming equality with God.

The discussion with the religious leaders continued and in John 10:37–38, Jesus said, 'If I am not doing the works of my Father, then do not believe me; but if I do them, even though you do not believe me, believe the works, that you may know and understand that the Father is in me and I am in the Father.' His statement is clear. We are forced into either rejecting Jesus completely as a liar or a madman, or accepting what he said about himself. There is more.

John 12:44–45 makes it clear that Jesus himself is the higher power, God the Son. It says, 'Jesus cried out and said, "He who believes in me, believes not in me but in him who sent me. And he who sees me sees him who sent me."'

Jesus is not a lesser god. As the Son, he is not less than, but the same substance as, the Father. I have a son and he is a human being also. This is part of what is meant by Jesus being the Son. When I believe in Jesus I believe in God; I believe in my higher power.

If anyone needs more convincing, there is John 14:6. Speaking to the apostle Thomas, Jesus said, 'I am the way, and the truth, and the life; no one comes to the Father, but by me.' If we would come to the Father, we must come to Jesus. Jesus is the Mediator, the one who stands between us and a holy God. We cannot approach the Father with unforgiven sin. We must come to Jesus, the Mediator between God and humankind. Jesus has taken our sin upon himself and made atonement for it. Without fear of punishment or rejection, we come to Jesus and he ushers us into the presence of the Father. That is why Jesus said that no one could come to the Father except through him.

Knowing how hard-headed and hard-hearted we are, I will go on just a little more. In John 15:23 Jesus said, 'He who hates me hates my Father also.' That may come as a bit of a shock. Could this be true? Notice Jesus did not say anything about a mere acknowledgement of the existence of God. You may move from atheism to agnosticism, and that is moving in the right direction, but it is not the same as faith in Jesus and love for God. The people to whom Jesus made this statement were convinced that they loved God, but they steadfastly rejected and hated Jesus. How could this be? The answer is that their religious observances were self-serving and not a reflection of a love for the God of Israel. They were engaged in religious ceremony and ritual — their hearts were unaffected. A love for God the Father will blossom, necessarily, into a love for God the Son.

In 1 John 2:22–23 we read, 'Who is the liar but he who denies that Jesus is the Christ? This is the antichrist, he who denies the Father and the Son. No one who denies the Son has the Father. He who confesses the Son has the Father also.' I hope you see the importance of this passage. To deny the Son is to become an antichrist, with a small 'a'. To deny that Jesus was the Christ amounts to a lie since the proof is there for any honest, open person to see. The miracles, the authority over the demonic kingdom, the fulfilling of the myriad of prophecies, are all clear proof to those who would see. But, those people, like us, had a problem that kept them in the dark. The good news is that when we trust in Jesus we are trusting in God, our higher power.

To those who have come to a place where they view God as only a higher power — I applaud you. At the same time, I invite you to cross the bridge and venture farther. It is not enough that God is a higher power, because a higher power never died on the cross for you. If your higher power would indeed be the God of creation, you will come to Jesus.

## A God you can understand

Alcoholics Anonymous is one of the most important institutions in the world. I fully support it. I also support other 12-step groups that have developed like Narcotics Anonymous. There is also an explicitly Christian 12-step programme called Overcomers Outreach. Hundreds of thousands of people are not only alive today, but are living better lives because of 12-step programmes. Many have begun their spiritual journey to Christ because of A.A.'s 12-steps, especially the eleventh step: 'Sought through prayer and meditation to improve our conscious contact with God, *as we understood him*, praying only for knowledge of his will for us and the power to carry that out.'

## A critique

People say, myself included, that some A.A. groups have assumed a place in the lives of the participants far greater than the founders, Bill W. and Dr Bob, envisioned. People have often reported to me that it is rare for Christianity to get any respect in actual meetings, in my region of California anyway. It is considered fine to be spiritual, even religious, but not blatantly Christian. This is unfortunate because Christian strength and experience may well be an important part of a person's sobriety. In addition, many A.A. people identify the group itself as their higher power. Accountability to a group or a sponsor may be necessary for sobriety early on, but this can take on a life of its own. The result can be the development of a quasi-cultic mentality. (Who in A.A. has not heard the 'Big Book' referred to as the 'A.A. Bible'?) In addition, when people leave A.A. or begin to attend fewer meetings, especially if Christian meetings are the alternative, there can be considerable criticism instead of support.

The main point I want to highlight here is something that has troubled me over the years: the little phrase 'as we understood him' found in the third and the eleventh steps. 'Higher power' is a weakened synonym for God and the phrase 'as we understood him' is fine, perhaps even necessary at first, but many never go beyond it.

The reason for the phrase was that A.A. needed to be inclusive. The programme was not intended to be a venue for Christian evangelism; rather the goal was and is sobriety. I think this is correct and as it should be. At the same time people have come up with some strange gods in A.A., 'door knob' and 'picture frame' come to mind, but the notion that a person will come to a correct understanding of God *on their own* is problematic. God is neither a doorknob nor a picture frame and we could do better with the real God. Even A.A. itself can become a god given the informal parameters for the 'higher power'. This is best illustrated by people who, in all seriousness, have said to me, 'I don't go to church, I go to A.A.'

How much does a drunk know about God? Not much probably. Not any more than anyone else. None of us knows anything about God by what we have figured out for ourselves. Usually what passes for knowledge of God is what we picked up or assimilated from around us: family, school, maybe church, or 'wisdom' that came out of a bottle. The God of our own understanding is not much of a God at all.

Fortunately, God has revealed himself in the Scripture. God is the Creator of all there is. He is holy, merciful, loving, just, all-knowing, all-powerful, all-present; and he sent his unique Son, Jesus the God-man, to die on a cross to redeem us. To believe in anything else is, from a biblical perspective, a form of idolatry. We will not get away with making up a God in our own image (Exod. 20:4). If I think God is a doorknob or a picture frame, I may get a few laughs in a meeting but I am on the road to becoming an idol worshipper. I know some people have started with God as a doorknob and have come around to seeing God for who he really is. But many do not; they get stuck with a false and weak God of their own creation.

Before they were alcoholics, alcoholics were sinners like everybody else. Their alcoholism caused them and their loved ones all kinds of grief, which is bad enough, but they were also rebelling and sinning against their Creator. Dealing with alcoholism is one thing; acknowledging sinfulness is another. A.A. is a mighty tool for sobriety, but only the God who sent his unique Son to die in the sinner's place forgives sin.

I am all for living a better, sober life, but a person is duped if he or she does not reckon with eternity. A.A. does not deal with eternal issues, only the here-and-now issues. The true and eternal God is the one we must go to. Let us remember what Jesus said in John 11:25: 'I am the resurrection and the life; he who believes in me, though he die, yet shall he live.'

Let me say to those who think they can believe in God, as they understand him: leave the idols and images and seek the God and Father of the Lord Jesus Christ. Give Jesus a chance. At the minimum, practise the principle articulated by Herbert Spencer found at the end of the second appendix, 'Spiritual Experience', in the 'Big Book' (p.570): 'There is a principle which is a bar against all information, which is proof against all arguments and which cannot fail to keep a man in everlasting ignorance — that principle is contempt prior to investigation.' Investigate the Bible. Find out who God really is and discover the depths that Jesus Christ went to for sinners like you and I.

# CHAPTER 14

# You have been duped if you think you cannot be tricked by the devil

N early everyone has the idea that he or she could spot the devil coming a mile away. If he arrived with horns, a pitchfork and dressed in fire-engine red, as the caricatures portray, everyone could. Occasionally the devil may make it easy for us but he is usually subtle, cunning, sophisticated and cultured — and we rarely see him coming. He is more deceiver than wizard or fire-breathing dragon.

## Tricked by the devil?

You might ask, 'How have I been tricked?' Have you been tricked into believing there is not a devil, or that God does not have an enemy whose goal it is to keep you from trusting in Jesus, like the Bible teaches? Have you been tricked into rejecting the notion of the reality of the devil's ultimate abode — hell itself? Have you been tricked into thinking that you do not need to have your sins forgiven, or that you can reject the Bible, the church and your conscience? Have you been tricked into thinking you are god, or will be reincarnated, or absorbed into the ocean of god-consciousness? Or, have you been tricked into thinking you are hopeless and beyond God's ability to forgive and rescue?

## A risk taken

It is clear to me that by merely referring to the devil I might discredit myself with many people. I might even be charged with being gullible. I remember what I used to think about those who were 'plagued with superstitious and childish ideas'.

You might say, 'This is the dawning of the third millennium, and are you going on with that medieval madness? Are you trying to frighten me into heaven with a "devil's gonna get you" approach?'

These charges would be warranted if there were no devil — and no hell and no demons. As a college student, my position was that devils and demons were simply mythological and a personification of human imperfections. Many people agree. But what if there is a devil, as the Bible says? What if Jesus was right, along with Paul, John and Peter?

Consider that most of the world's religions have depictions of devils and demons somewhere in their literature. Are these diabolic characters not pictured in religious art around the world? The occult world itself, with its mediums, channellers, sorcerers, witches, wizards and the like, attests to the world of evil spirits, demons and devils.

Does our common human experience not illustrate the existence of evil? Is there not something outside of all that is human — something that is twisted, corrupt and polluted? From time to time, we get the sense of this 'otherness'. Wicked though we may be, there yet lurks a foreign presence in our personal and corporate world that is foul and unclean, and is distinct from humanity. What I am referring to is what the Bible calls the devil. Certainly, admitting the existence of evil is not the same as believing in devils and demons. While many admit to the reality of evil, fewer acknowledge real evil entities. But can there be one without the other?

The collective witness of the New Testament is that there is an actual entity called Satan or the devil. We can all attest to the existence of evil, whether human or demonic in origin, but Jesus and his apostles also spoke of Satan, a separate and distinct, non-human and supernatural enemy of God.

## The devil's bad press

Some years ago, a mother murdered her five children with the hope that she would save them from the 'fires of hell'. In her confusion, she reasoned that if she killed her children before they went completely wild she would be doing them a favour.

Unstable people have long blamed the devil for their shameful deeds. I am sure you have seen desperately ill people wandering the streets of large cities shouting or mumbling nonsense about the devil. The mad ravings of lunatics are often filled with references to Satan and other notorious characters, and the effect is that many of us attribute the existence of the devil solely to the deranged imaginings of the mentally ill.

Will we allow the devil's bad press to determine our view of his actual existence? Madmen rave about Napoleon, Abraham Lincoln, Adolph Hitler, Elvis Presley, even Jesus, but we do not doubt the existence of these people. My point is that we are tempted to reject the reality of the devil because of these associations with mental instability. The simple fact that the devil finds his way into the delusions of those who unhappily suffer from mental illness, is no reason to dismiss his reality. We must not allow the devil's bad press to determine our theology, for if we do, we may end up being duped.

## Can the devil trick us?

Who likes to be told that the devil has tricked them? Let me appeal to you: Do not make up your mind too quickly. After all, you do not know if there is, or is not, a devil. You cannot prove it one way or another. Consider how much you have to lose if you are wrong. If there is not a devil, you have lost nothing, but if there is a devil, you risk more than you can ever imagine.

To think that we cannot be tricked illustrates our pride — we place too much confidence in our intellectual or spiritual capacities and abilities. I know it may be a leap for some to believe in the existence of Satan, yet, no one can prove there is *not* a devil. Can I, on the other hand, prove there is one? No, I cannot demonstrate it sufficiently to convince most people. However, I have encountered the devil many times, up-close and personal, as Jesus did, and so have countless thousands of Christians over the centuries. These testimonies count for something.

There is another reason people are reluctant to admit the reality of the devil and demons — the subject of hell follows closely behind. To admit one reality is tantamount to admitting the other, and hell is the really big issue. Could it be that people will close their eyes to the objective reality of Satan in order to avoid having to face the truth of hell?

## Basis of authority

This chapter on Satan and his deceptive practices is based upon the Scripture. I also have my own experiences as a Christian and a pastor to rely upon, experiences that are typical of Christians throughout the ages. I appeal to two witnesses, then — the Bible and experience, but the greater of these is the Bible. Although I have encountered hundreds of demons over the course of nearly four decades of ministry, and despite these encounters mirroring those described in both Scripture and ancient and modern church history, my primary appeal is to Scripture. Here first, however, is my own experience.

## My personal experience

The bulk of my experience with the demonic world took place during the Jesus Movement of the late 1960s and early 1970s. I continue to observe demons in action, but for some reason, such encounters are now more infrequent. In the years directly preceding the Jesus Movement and throughout its duration (1967–1972), there was a tremendous interest in and involvement with the occult and mystical Eastern religions. As a result, those of us who ministered to 'counter-culture people' were forced to deal with demonic activity. This is because participation in occult practices and the submission of the will to false gods often opens the door to demonic activity. For example, people who acquired the ability to communicate with 'spirits' would sometimes discover these spiritual entities were actually demons. The apostle Paul, in his first letter to the Corinthian church, in regard to offerings made to idols, said, 'What pagans sacrifice they offer to demons and not to God' (1 Cor. 10:20).

I attest to the reality of Satan. He is indeed real, and besides that singular entity, there are legions of demons who serve under Satan's leadership. These demonic spirits normally conceal themselves; they do not like their existence to be widely known. But there have been times in history, particularly when there were tremendous outpourings of God's Holy Spirit, where Satan engaged in a kind of counter-attack and revealed himself. And, of course, that is what happened in the Jesus Movement. It caught me by surprise, since I doubted the existence of the devil at first, but when it became a part of my own experience, I had to change my theology.

## Jesus and the devil

Jesus acknowledged the existence of Satan. He not only spoke about Satan but he cast demons out as a regular part of his ministry. His disciples and also his enemies were amazed at his authority over demons. Jesus was no wizard, shaman or magician. He simply expelled demons with a word. Jesus employed no incantation, no ritual, no ceremony. He merely cast out demons with a command. It is the integrity of Jesus that matters most to me. The authority Jesus had over unclean spirits — simple, powerful and permanent — speaks volumes to me about the nature and reality of demonic forces.

Jesus authorized his disciples to cast out demons, which they did, and it became a regular feature of their ministry. Jesus first sent out the twelve apostles (Luke 9:1–6) and then a larger group of seventy. This last group reported back to Jesus, 'Lord, even the demons are subject to us in your name' (Luke 10:17). And so it has been ever since — this even became a part of my ministry during the Jesus Movement, and to a lesser extent, it continues to this day.

## The text: Genesis 3:1–7

Already in the first few chapters of the Bible, there is an account dealing with the creature we have come to call the devil or Satan. 'Now the serpent was more subtle than any other wild creature that the Lord God had made' (Gen. 3:1). The serpent is identified as Satan in Revelation 12:9: 'And the great dragon was thrown down, that ancient serpent, who is called the Devil and Satan, the deceiver of the whole world — he was thrown down to the earth, and his angels were thrown down with him.'

We do not know how Satan appeared as a serpent in the garden of Eden. Perhaps Satan possessed a serpent as a 'spirit' possesses and speaks through mediums. Notice that the serpent is described as subtle in Genesis and a deceiver in Revelation. Satan is a created being, and is intelligent, crafty and persuasive. Revelation depicts a magnificent creature who was cast out of God's presence along with 'his angels' or demons (Rev. 12:7–12). This passage chronicles the origin of the demonic realm. This creature is still able to trick us, as he did in the Genesis account.

Satan (in the form of a serpent) was present in the garden where Adam and Eve lived. They were the first humans made in the image of God. Although they had a personal relationship with God, they were still tricked. This must give us pause.

Genesis 3:1 reads: 'He said to the woman, "Did God say, 'You shall not eat of any tree of the garden'?"' God had told them not to eat of one particular tree, the tree of the knowledge of good and evil. The actual quotation is: 'You may freely eat of every tree of the garden; but of the tree of the knowledge of good and evil you shall not eat, for in the day that you eat of it you shall die' (Gen. 2:16–17). Adam and Eve were only forbidden to eat of this one tree, and if they did they would die.

The serpent's original question dealt with 'any tree', while the command had to do with only one special tree. Satan started out with a half-truth, and Eve corrected him when she pointed out that only one tree was involved. Eve, however, was not completely clear on the issue because she said to the serpent, 'We may eat of the fruit of the trees of the garden; but God said, "You shall not eat of the fruit of the tree which is in the midst of the garden, neither shall you touch it, lest you die"' (Gen. 3:3). The statement about touching the tree was not part of the original command. Already there is error, and a little error can lead to a big error. The problem was only just beginning.

'But the serpent said to the woman, "You will not die. For God knows that when you eat of it your eyes will be opened, and you will be like God, knowing good and evil"' (Gen. 3:4–5). Satan directly contradicts what God had declared — death as the penalty for breaking his command. Satan lies again in attributing false motives to God. Satan intimates that God did not want Adam and Eve to acquire knowledge because it would give them a godlike status. What a powerful incentive for the woman this was: 'You will be like God.' Of course, that was Satan's original problem. He wanted to be like God, and his rebellion against God's authority was the reason for his expulsion from heaven. This is also the human condition. We are tempted to be something other than who and what we are.

The story continues: 'So when the woman saw that the tree was good for food, and that it was a delight to the eyes, and that the tree was to be desired to make one wise, she took of its fruit and ate; and she also gave some to her husband, and he ate' (Gen. 3:6). Note the three incentives for Eve. One is food, or what the Bible in another place calls the 'lust of the flesh'. The second is beauty, or the 'lust of the eyes' and the third is knowledge and power, or the 'pride of life'. I am comparing the Genesis passage to something the apostle John spoke of in a letter he wrote to churches in A.D. 96 (1 John 2:16).

The need or desire for food, beauty or knowledge is not wrong. These are necessary for life. But the acquisition of these things will not make anyone 'like God' despite what the serpent affirmed. Adam and Eve had all they needed in their relationship with their Creator and in what he had provided for them. Lust and pride drove them to crave more. The serpent created a psychological or spiritual vacuum for those first humans and manipulated them into thinking that satisfaction could be found in their immediate environment. It reminds me of advertising, which creates desire for products that promise health, wealth, love, pleasure and power — but which we eventually discover are never able to satisfy. Perhaps Satan works similarly today in enticing us to seek after that which will only disappoint and which will one day deliver death rather than life.

Already in the garden, the same temptations we all face and succumb to were present. There is 'nothing new under the sun'. Not being a 'god', Eve was vulnerable and was no match for the serpent — just as we are no match for the wiles of the devil today. Beware imagining you are an exception.

## The dying of Adam and Eve

The narrative continues: 'Then the eyes of both were opened, and they knew that they were naked; and they sewed fig leaves together and made themselves aprons' (Gen. 3:7). Adam and Eve did not become like God at all. Suddenly, possessing knowledge of sin, their sexuality was twisted and they were no longer innocent. They had been naked with each other in the garden all along, but as soon as they knew the difference between good and evil, they hid themselves and sewed fig leaves to hide their nakedness.

The Creator God, knowing of their transgression, sought out the fallen couple, not to condemn them but to restore them. They responded, however, like we often do and hid themselves. Refusing to confess and repent, they were expelled from the garden and cast away from God's presence. In other words, they experienced spiritual death. The death that God said they would experience if they disobeyed his command was a spiritual death. Physical death is bad enough, but the real problem is spiritual death, the reality of which Satan wants to conceal from us.

How many and varied are the attempts we devise to deny the reality of eternal or spiritual death, much less physical death. Consider reincarnation. It proposes a constant recycling of life and death. Or, another concept based on Hindu thought teaches that life and death are maya or illusion. There is the Greek notion that the 'soul' simply lives on and on. There is also the concept of annihilation: that the grave is the end of existence.

Satan lied, 'You won't die.' It was only a half-truth since they did not, at that point, experience physical death. Likewise, when we sin, we do not immediately drop dead. But sin always results in spiritual separation from God. In the Genesis story, this is illustrated with Adam and Eve being barred from the garden and being sent 'east of Eden'. They no longer enjoyed personal fellowship with God.

We do ourselves an injustice by crediting ourselves with greater wisdom than we actually possess. We do ourselves great damage by rejecting the existence of an evil presence, loose in the universe, that is more powerful, smarter and wiser than we are. Satan was able to trick Eve. She relied upon her own abilities rather than trusting in the commands of God. Adam also disobeyed what God said. Adam knew the command as well, yet he was very easily taken in by what Eve had to say, and she was not even a crafty serpent.

## Angel of light

Satan — deceptive, subtle, alluring, giver of knowledge, beauty and 'godliness'. This portrayal of the devil from the Old Testament we also observe in the New Testament. For example, in his second letter to the church at Corinth, Paul spoke of some 'apostles' who were causing a great deal of confusion. It is not clear exactly what their message was, but it was spiritual, religious and sounded like orthodox Christian teaching. Here is Paul's warning: 'For such men are false apostles, deceitful workmen, disguising themselves as apostles of Christ. And no wonder, for even Satan disguises himself as an angel of light. So it is not strange if his servants also disguise themselves as servants of right-eousness' (2 Cor. 11:13–15).

This text reminds us of Satan in the garden. Paul uses powerful words — 'deceitful', 'disguises' — which reveal to us that Satan had not changed much over the centuries. Satan disguised himself as an apostle of Christ, and perhaps had quite a following in the Corinthian church.

The devil is at work inside the church as well as outside of it. It is like terrorism. There are no front lines and the enemy has many faces — this is the nature of the spiritual battle. Satan's most effective tactic is to infiltrate the opposing forces, and this is what happened in Corinth. The devil had his advocates right there in that church — his troops *looked like* servants of righteousness. This is often the case. Satan's deceivers may even appear more holy, religious and spiritually correct than the genuine members of the church they have infiltrated. The Corinthian believers were not able to distinguish between the true and the false. They were taken in; they were tricked; they were duped. And so it may be with us.

Do you think that because we live over two thousand years from the events that Paul wrote about, somehow we are spiritually or intellectually superior? Even a cursory examination of human history is revealing. Many things have changed over time but this has not. Frequently, men and women are not spiritually discerning.

Satan disguises himself as an angel of light. Would Satan be effective if he declared: 'I am the devil. I hate you. I am against you. I am the enemy of God and I want you to follow me'?

To illustrate my contention that Satan is a master at disguise I would call your attention to the many groups founded by 'beings' who professed to be angels, usually the archangel Gabriel or the archangel Michael, and declared that they possess new and improved truth. How many world religions and Christian-based cults trace their origin to some spiritual creature announcing itself to be an angel or some other exalted entity? Evil spirits will even impersonate Jesus himself. When these appear in light, beauty and majesty, they are so persuasive that deception is almost guaranteed.

## Clever packaging — angels of light

Packaging is everything these days. *The Pacific Sun* and *The San Francisco Weekly*, local tabloids, both ran stories about health gurus who professed to be able to make people beautiful, strong, popular and sexy. There were assurances that they could clear away emotional and spiritual blockages through the proper use of stress reduction, acupuncture, visualizations, diet, yoga, meditation, and so on. Deep massage bodywork and homeopathic medicine were part of their arsenal too. The promises were packaged quite well — it was not going to cost very much and results would be quickly achieved.

What I am referring to here is not necessarily demonic in nature, but those who are struggling in life, whose health is failing, who are experiencing emotional distress and confusion — these are the ones who are most open to deception. Our greed, our lusts, our fears, and our lack of satisfaction lead us to embrace concepts that are antithetical to the truth of God. Even if not outright demonic, the outcome is the same — deception.

## Guru power

Living in the San Francisco Bay area, I have become well acquainted with alternative spiritualities and the New Age movement. Some of the brightest and most well-educated people imaginable have, for example, become deeply devoted to forms of yoga and Zen meditation and have devoted years to a sincere searching after God and truth. Many of these people have become devotees of gurus, some home-grown and others imported from India. Some spiritual teachers, it is claimed, perform miracles, often with just a touch. *Shakti* is the power touch employed by some of these gurus. It is said to bring enlightenment and initiate incredible emotional and spiritual change in a person. This is powerful and profound; it is also convincing and persuasive. Basically, however, it is a lie. Satan is powerful and able to work certain kinds of miracles, and it is my contention that the *shakti* power of these gurus is demonic in nature. Muktananda, Sai Baba and Osho, among others, had this kind of power. I doubt that even these gurus knew where the power was coming from or its exact nature. Thousands are yet under the sway of the power gurus.

## The father of lies

The Gospel of John records a confrontation Jesus had with some Jewish leaders. These men asserted that they were descendants of Abraham, meaning they were quite *kosher*. Jesus said to them, 'If you were Abraham's children, you would do what Abraham did, but now you seek to kill me, a man who has told you the truth which I heard from God; this is not what Abraham did. You do what your father did' (John 8:39–41).

The leaders countered Jesus by saying, 'We were not born of fornication; we have one Father, even God' (John 8:41). They meant, on the one hand, that they were in good standing with God. But they were also accusing Jesus of illegitimacy — that his conception was the result of fornication, not legitimate sex between a husband and a wife. It had apparently already been circulated that there was some question as to exactly who Jesus' father was. They did not understand the virgin birth, and neither Mary nor Joseph ever cleared up the issue. Jesus never dealt with it either; rather he left it to his biographers, Matthew and Luke, to set the record straight.

Jesus replied, 'If God were your Father, you would love me, for I proceeded and came forth from God; I came not of my own accord, but he sent me. Why do you not understand what I say? It is because you cannot bear to hear my word' (John 8:42–43). As an aside, let me say that the degree to which we cannot stand to hear the message of Jesus is the measure of how extensively we have been deceived.

Then Jesus said, 'You are of your father, the devil, and your will is to do your father's desires. He was a murderer from the beginning, and has nothing to do with the truth, because there is no truth in him. When he lies, he speaks according to his own nature, for he is a liar and the father of lies' (John 8:44). The point Jesus makes is that Satan is a liar. His whole purpose is to keep others from knowing and following the truth.

## Big lies and little lies

There are big lies and then there are little lies. Among the little ones, I think of astrology — the idea that the stars and planets control our destiny. Or, that we live many lives, returning perhaps as a microbe, then maybe as a toad, then maybe as a dog, and then maybe, by virtue of paying off bad karma, coming back as a human being. I think of lies such as that Jesus is only the God of the Christians, Jesus visited India or China or Persia during the so-called 'lost years', or the conviction that the church edited reincarnation out of the Bible. There was also the story that the disciples stole the body of Jesus from the tomb and merely fabricated his resurrection.

There are many more little lies, like those told by the mediums and the psychics that we find in books such as the Course in Miracles or the Urantia Book. There is a popular notion that there are good spirits and bad spirits and that the bad spirits must be avoided and the good spirits appeased. Actually, this is really a big lie, since it might just be the most widespread religious concept the world has known. It might also be expressed as the belief in luck, or fortune, and the constant and anxiety-producing effort to have good luck.

Of the big lies, I will mention only two. From these two lies, most others flow. One has to do with who Jesus is and the other has to do with what Jesus did.

## The first big lie

The first big lie has to do with who Jesus actually is. Jesus is always the main issue. Those who do not accept the biblical account of Jesus' person essentially *demote* him. He becomes a great teacher, an angel, a spiritually evolved being, a transcended master, a failed reformer, the founder of a religion, a charismatic but delusional young man, a clever magician, and more.

Here is a summary of who Jesus is. The Scripture is abundantly clear that Jesus Christ is Emmanuel, God in the flesh. We do not understand this because it does not seem reasonable to us that God should or could become human. However, there is no way to get around the fact that this is what the Bible teaches, Old and New Testament alike. Do you think Christians would make something like this up in light of all the trouble it has caused over the centuries? If we would capitulate and reduce Jesus to just a good teacher, great prophet or fantastic guy, we would fit right in with everyone else. But we cannot deny what the Scripture asserts. Why?

Because to be the perfect sacrifice for sin the Messiah had to be perfect, and only God is perfect. Besides Jesus being God, he is man, too. Since God cannot die, Jesus must be fully man to die. This is the paradoxical picture of Jesus: he is fully God and fully man. Everything that Jesus did depends on who he is. The biblical view of Jesus requires us to hold these two realities in tension even though they seem, at times, to contradict each other.

## The second big lie

The second big lie has to do with what Jesus did. He is often transformed into merely an example of sacrificial love. He was a loving person who taught the world the great lessons of giving and humbleness. His 'do unto others' is admired and highlighted, as is his emphasis on forgiveness, but this is the extent of it. The great work of Jesus is essentially ignored.

Here is a summary of what Jesus did. The God-man, the Messiah of Israel, the perfect and sinless, sacrificial and passover Lamb of God, went willingly to the cross, suffered and took the punishment for our sin upon himself, died in our place, and on the third day rose from the dead. He revealed himself to the apostles and a great many others, and then ascended to the Father in heaven. From heaven he will one day return to receive all who have trusted in him as Lord and Saviour. Jesus satisfied the just demands of a holy God who cannot tolerate sin. Jesus took the punishment that is due to sinners upon himself, shed his own blood and earned our forgiveness. Without the sacrifice of Jesus on the cross there is no possibility of the forgiveness of sin. Jesus triumphed over sin, death and the devil.

## We have all been duped

We have all believed lies from the devil. They come to us through cultural myths, things that we just accept, or concepts that we embrace without critical analysis. I was as vulnerable as anyone else. Probably the biggest lie I bought into was the idea that aliens would show up in UFOs and would prove that Christianity was just a great hoax. Sometimes I am embarrassed to admit this; I mention it thinking there might be someone out there like me.

If you look carefully at yourself, you will probably discover that, like most of us, one or more of Satan's lies has already tricked you to one degree or another. I am not interested in demeaning anybody, but wisdom would have it that we admit the possibility that we have, at some point and in some way, already been duped by the devil.

## The veiling — a concluding thought

Consider Paul's words to the Corinthian church: 'And even if our gospel is veiled, it is veiled only to those who are perishing. In their case the god of this world has blinded the minds of the unbelievers, to keep them from seeing the light of the gospel of the glory of Christ, who is the likeness of God' (2 Cor. 4:3–4).

Conversion means, among other things, that we recognize the truth about who Jesus is. Prior to conversion we are blinded, we can neither see who Jesus is nor understand what he did. It is as though a veil had been thrown over our face, covering our eyes, so that we are blinded.

The veiling metaphor contains a great and awful truth. Satan, the 'god of this world', is the one who veils and blinds. Here is a picture of the adversary, the enemy of God, taking the most natural course to win the cosmic struggle — blind, deceive and confuse, so that the light of the saving gospel of Jesus cannot be seen. Satan's ultimate intent is to deceive us as to who Jesus is and what Jesus did. This is the heart of it. When we see who Jesus is and what he did, we will want to become his followers. It really is as simple as this.

Why would Satan have an interest in tricking Adam and Eve? Why would Satan have an interest in tricking you? Because he is Satan. The name means 'adversary'. He is at war with God. A spiritual war is going on throughout the universe. It is a war between good and evil. Sometimes we see it lived out in history and world events. Sometimes we experience it in our own lives; indeed, the conflict goes on even within us.

Satan tricks us because he hates us and wants to separate us for ever from the God who made us. Satan is the instigator of murder, suicide and war. The ultimate blinding is hiding or distorting the truth of who Jesus is and what he did.

Jesus, the Light of the world, can penetrate, overwhelm and overcome darkness. He can open the eyes of the blind. The light of Jesus and the truth of the cross and the resurrection overcome darkness and bring light and life. Be deceived no longer.

# CHAPTER 15

# You have been duped if...
# (five shorter subjects)

My editor says, 'You have been duped if you think you have read your last chapter.' I admit to adding a few additional subjects and lumping them together in this last chapter. Although their treatment is brief, a book on being 'duped' would not be complete without touching on these final topics.

Before we consider the five shorter subjects, let me ask again: Do we know what we are doing? While on the cross Jesus uttered these words: 'Father, forgive them; for they know not what they do' (Luke 23:34). This is how we are: we do not know what we are doing. We, the duped ones, go our own way and continue to rebel against God and his law. We work against our own good. We would not do so if we knew what we were doing.

Why do we reject the God who loves us? Perhaps we have rejected the church as we know it, God as we have come to understand him or Christianity as we have experienced it, but who would knowingly reject a gracious and compassionate Saviour?

## First: You have been duped if you think aliens are going to prove Christianity is a fraud

Now why would I pick such a topic? Well, I personally fell for this. Maybe some of you are fascinated with the idea of UFOs, or are at least avid science-fiction fans. Maybe in the back of your mind you wonder if the God of the Bible is only a local deity, maybe the product of the 'earthling mind', and that 'superior' organisms, somewhere out there, know better.

I got hooked on the movie *The Invasion of the Body Snatchers*. In my view, the remake of that movie, with Donald Sutherland, was even better than the original. The original version came out in 1959 when I was a very impressionable teenager. Under the influence of this sci-fi film, I began to think that aliens would arrive and prove that Christianity was a big fraud.

Our culture has drilled into us the acceptance of aliens. Think of it: *Star Trek, Close Encounters of the Third Kind, Star Wars*, the *Alien* series, *ET* and many others — they have conditioned us to accept the existence of intelligent life elsewhere in the universe. More than that, we have UFO cults, some of whose adherents get excited about the myths surrounding Roswell, New Mexico, where an alien spacecraft is supposed to have crashed. (The government is thought to be safeguarding the alien remains.) I suppose a large number of Americans believe there are aliens out there that might show up at any time. This might influence a person's view of Jesus; it certainly did my own.

## SETI

Attraction to the existence of aliens is not for eccentrics alone. Consider the effort on the part of the scientific community called SETI, the Search for Extra-Terrestrial Intelligence. Laser beams and radio signals are being sent into the nether regions with the hope of making contact with whatever life might be out there. Well-meaning people are determined to make contact with, or find evidence of, intelligent life somewhere else in the universe.

As yet, there has been no contact and I doubt there ever will be. It is interesting that Charles Haddon Spurgeon, the great English Baptist preacher of the latter part of the nineteenth century and an amateur astronomer, was not concerned about the possibility of life elsewhere than earth. *Why I am a Christian* (Evangelical Press, 2002) contains an essay I wrote in which I quote Spurgeon on this point. Someone asked Spurgeon if he expected to find life on Mars and he replied (author's paraphrase), 'It wouldn't surprise me one bit.' His point was that God is the Creator of the universe, and there is nowhere that he does not reign as Lord. So, Spurgeon reasoned, if life is discovered somewhere else, we will find that it owes its existence to the very same God who revealed himself in Scripture.

Some people are excited about the possibility of microbes being discovered on Mars. If that were so, would it come as a shock? After all, the same laws of physics, chemistry, and so on, apply throughout the universe. The strong and weak nuclear forces, gravity and electro-magnetism are universal. But some people will uncritically accept what is in fact an unproven speculation and conclude that if any life form is found other than on earth, however primitive, it will prove there is no God.

## Evolution and time

I will pursue this subject one step further and briefly describe an aspect of my view of evolution. I do so knowing that some Christians will reject my argument, and perhaps my Christianity as well, but I want to state that it is possible to be a Bible-believing Christian and not discard all evolutionary concepts.

Science keeps pushing back the time when human life appeared on the planet. It used to be 40,000 years and then it was 75,000 years. That date was moved back to 100,000, and just recently, some were willing to go back a million years. One million years ago, it is conjectured, there were creatures who walked upright, had large brains and were intelligent. It is claimed these 'humans' were not only capable of thought, but left behind primitive forms of art and religion as well.

The problem is that some people will think, 'The Bible demands a short history for both the creation of the world and human beings. Therefore, the ancient history of the universe proves that the Bible is wrong.' Or, some might reason, 'Since we see that life forms change, since we see fossil evidence for the evolving of organic life, the Bible has got to be wrong.' However, it matters neither when advanced 'human' forms appeared nor what abilities they had. It does not matter that the universe is 13.7 billion years old and that the earth has been around at least five billion years. The issue is not anatomical likeness; it is not the capacity to make tools, do art or engage in abstract reasoning. The issue does not have anything to do with dates and times, rather the issue is creation in the image of God.

How God created, or when he created — these are details. Perhaps God's creation of the first humans in his image is recent, or ancient. It does not matter. Personally, I think intelligence, or better, self-awareness and abstract reasoning capacity, goes with being created in the image of God. However, let us not be duped into thinking that science, aliens or logical philosophical models prove that the biblical revelation is false.

## Second: You have been duped if you no longer care about yourself

I imagine that some of us, at some point in our lives, have experienced self-loathing. There was a time in my life (1980–1982) when I struggled in a way I never imagined I would. In fact, I felt as if I did not care about myself any more. Maybe you can remember a time in your own life when you felt that way.

A significant personal loss can have a radical impact on the way we feel about ourselves. For example, a traumatic event occurs — a death in the family, a divorce, a severe injury, the termination of a job, the family home burns down — and the result is that you do not care what happens to you. This is a dangerous time emotionally, spiritually and physically.

You may not literally say to yourself that you no longer care, but unconsciously you begin to live your life as if you do not. You take risks that you normally would not. You make commitments that would have been inconceivable before. You become accident-prone and may experience thoughts of suicide. You simply give up on yourself; you give up on life. Perhaps depression takes hold of you. The whole thing can drive you right into the ground.

## A terrible trilogy

Our text is John 10:10. It is a shocking verse. Jesus said, 'The thief comes only to steal and kill and destroy.' The context of this passage is pastoral — sheep, sheepfold, shepherd and sheep-stealer. Sheepfolds of that day were made from field rocks piled up only a few feet high. Sheep would be brought into the folds each night through a single narrow entrance and they were then relatively safe from predators. The low wall had no razor wire or other impediment, so it was possible to climb over it, and every once in a while a thief would steal one of the sheep.

What can be stolen from us that would have tragic consequences? Consider this: What happens when we lose hope? What happens when our dreams are crushed and our future looks bleak? What happens when our strength fails and injury and disease become a permanent part of our life? What happens when we are buried beneath a load of guilt and shame? When the thief steals something that is so central to our life, we are tempted to feel that we do not care about ourselves. And just in case you think more highly of yourself than you ought, be warned that the thief will surely come knocking on your door.

The thief comes to 'steal and kill and destroy'. Notice the sequence. To 'kill' is next in line. We are driven towards death, sometimes slowly, sometimes quickly. Satan has been a murderer from the beginning. He is a warrior who delights when armies slaughter each other; he is a promoter of genocide and suicide. Yes, there are the human elements — politics, economics, sociology, psychology, religion — but draw back the curtain, and you will observe that Satan is often pulling the strings behind the scenes. Satan is counting on death to put the unconverted for ever beyond hope. As the writer of Hebrews said, 'It is appointed for men to die once, and after that comes judgement' (Heb. 9:27).

'Destroy' comes last. Jesus is not using redundant language either; kill and destroy are different. Destroy means eternal ruin — complete, final, infinite — and this is the goal of the thief. It is not enough to steal and kill. These are merely the initial steps. This terrible trilogy is not the end of the story, for Jesus had much more to say.

## The Good Shepherd

'I came that they may have life, and have it abundantly' (John 10:10). To those who have come to a place, for whatever reason, where they no longer care about themselves, I would say, 'Remember that Jesus came to bring you life. If you give up now, you will miss it.' The old saying is well worth taking to heart: Never give up!

When you begin to feel worthless and come to view the world as a terrible place, you become blinded and trapped in your own despair. I hope that if you have had that experience you will see something else. I repeat, Jesus has come that you might have life and have it abundantly.

Jesus is saying, 'You are not beyond hope. You are not worthless. There is more life than you can imagine waiting for you.' Do not give up. You have yet to experience the forgiveness of your sin. It is absolutely wonderful to know that you are forgiven and to know you are free. Some people have broken all of God's commandments. Some even hate to see their reflection in a mirror. Some prefer to live as hermits because they feel so dreadful about themselves. Many people struggle along feeling unfulfilled, unsatisfied, sometimes miserable and usually disappointed. If this description fits you, hear it again: You can have meaning in your life. You can wake up with something good to do tomorrow, and the day after that, and on and on. You can know who God is; you can know you have a home in heaven. This is not pie-in-the-sky nonsense; I am not saying that all your problems will vanish. What I declare is based on what Jesus Christ said. He said, 'I came that they may have life, and have it abundantly.' Do not let the thief run off with your abundant life.

## Third: You have been duped if you think you will be happy in hell

This statement is a form of common bravado. In Mark Twain's *Huckleberry Finn*, Huck Finn decides he is going to turn in his new friend Jim, a runaway slave. He is in tremendous conflict about it. Finally, he concludes, 'I am not going to turn Jim in, even if I go to hell' (author's paraphrase). Perhaps Huck thought he could be happy in hell, or at least he was resigned to the idea of it. Does anyone *really* think they would be happy in hell?

'Well, so what? Who cares for the consequences?' Are these strong words, uttered by a person with all his wits about him, with all options considered and all eventualities calculated? 'So I go to hell; what does it matter?' Are these rash words? Have you ever said such things?

To take it a step further, some say, 'Well, at least I will be with some of my friends in hell.' This is moving from resignation to a greater delusion. It is true, but it will not be like being with your friends in the old days. I do not know how many people believe this lie. Today, it is likely that more people believe there is no hell than believe there is one. Perhaps dismissing the possibility of hell is little more than a desperate hope that it does not exist. To believe that you would be happy in hell, just in case there is one, is making a poor peace with the most awful prospect we could ever know.

## A few facts about hell

Hell, as I have articulated before, is essentially separation from God. The divide between heaven and hell has been described as 'The Great Divorce' (C. S. Lewis). Hell is a permanent separation from all that is good. Married people who are having trouble in their relationship may agree to a trial separation. There is no 'trial' with hell — it is everlasting. Once in hell, there is no reconciliation, no 'getting back together'.

No one knows for sure what hell is like. Biblical commentators, even those who take the Bible seriously, do not agree on whether the images of hell depicted in the Bible are to be taken literally. It is a complicated subject. Despite the differences of opinion and interpretation, I am convinced hell is very real. To be sure, if I could get around the idea of hell, or make it less awful, I would. If I could somehow salve the mangled sensibilities of those who absolutely recoil from the notion of hell, I would. However, it would be a great mistake. The Scripture makes it very clear: hell is far more dreadful than the images that fire and brimstone convey.

It is important to grasp that there is logic to the existence of hell. Begin with the fact that God is holy and righteous. This means, among other things, that sin cannot enter his presence. The sinner must either be forgiven or be excluded from God's presence for ever. This is what I mean by hell being a logical and, I might add, a necessary doctrine. If I were to die with unforgiven sin, then I would go to hell. It is as simple as that.

When Satan rebelled against God in heaven, he was banished. The Bible teaches that hell was actually created for Satan and his angels because, as rebels, they could no longer be in God's presence. Sin cannot be in God's presence. So hell is the place of separation for those whose sin has not been forgiven.

## Adjusting

I was once given a book written by a death-row inmate at San Quentin. He spent many years in the adjustment centre, a prison within a prison. The book confirmed something I had learned from reading stories of the Holocaust. (The work of Victor Frankel comes to mind.) Even in the worst of places, people will adjust in order to survive. For example, Richard Wurmbrand, a Christian pastor, survived and remained emotionally and spiritually intact despite the worst conditions the Soviets could devise. He was able to make adjustments and survive. The same would be true of hell as well. Its occupants would adjust to a life without light and hope and love.

## Images of hell

The images of hell in the Scripture are dramatic. Some Christians take them very literally; some take them more figuratively, as I have already mentioned. I make no judgement on how you want to interpret the images of hell found in the Bible. Some people find ways to be rid of hell altogether. However, that would be a mistake. In fact, I cannot even join with those who hold a 'wider mercy' concept and pardon the so-called innocents — those who have never heard the gospel. Despite the negative aspects of the doctrine of hell, and despite its unpopularity, it is very clearly present in Scripture. If I did deny the reality of hell, or somehow minimize it, I would only be deceiving you.

Fire is one of the dramatic images of hell. In Revelation 19:20 and 20:10, reference is made to a 'lake of fire'. In Mark 9, Jesus spoke three times of the 'fire of hell'. Mark records: 'And if your eye causes you to sin, pluck it out; it is better for you to enter the kingdom of God with one eye than with two eyes to be thrown into hell, where their worm does not die, and the fire is not quenched' (Mark 9:47–48). This fire, not necessary for life and health, is one that does not consume, but is eternal.

Another image of hell is darkness. We find this in a number of places (Matt. 8:12; 22:13; 25:30). Teaching about the great and final judgement, Jesus said, 'And cast the worthless servant into the outer darkness; there men will weep and gnash their teeth' (Matt. 25:30). What Jesus meant by 'outer' probably has to do with endless or eternal darkness. The weeping and gnashing of teeth is a figure of speech designed to describe extreme pain and suffering. What a grim picture this is! In Luke 13:28, Jesus said, 'There you will weep and gnash your teeth, when you see Abraham and Isaac and Jacob and all the prophets in the kingdom of God and you yourselves thrust out.' How can darkness and fire coexist? The very question demonstrates that we may not have as complete an understanding of hell as we would like, and are therefore not required to adopt a literal interpretation.

These images of hell make me shudder. I hate to think of anyone going to hell. I know some very fine people that I have loved and cared for, who it is more than likely have gone there. If I reject the doctrine of hell on their account, hoping that if I did they would somehow be spared, this would only be wishful thinking. Sounder logic prevents me from doing this. Hell exists because God is holy. Rejection of God is a rebellion of infinite proportions and demands an infinite punishment. I am not in charge of heaven or hell; my wishes do not count. It is better to acknowledge the truth and trust in the power of God to save those whom he calls.

## The parable of the rich man and Lazarus

The most complete description we have of hell is found in the parable of the rich man and Lazarus (Luke 16:19–31). Here is a brief summary of the parable. A rich man died and went to hell. A sick old man named Lazarus, who had routinely begged for food outside the rich man's home, died and went to heaven. (Lazarus did not go to heaven because he was poor any more than the rich man went to hell because he was rich.) The rich man pleaded with God to send Lazarus to him with a drop of water to ease his suffering. Then, the rich man pleaded with God to send someone to his family members so that they would avoid having to come to the place of torment he was in. But, and this is a main point of the parable, no one could cross a deep chasm that separated heaven from hell.

We find several characteristics of hell in the parable. Those who inhabit hell are conscious, capable of complex reasoning and even have a concern that others should not end up there. They have a semblance of their humanity intact. They are in a place of punishment, but the most dramatic point is that hell is permanent separation — there is no way out. The person in hell, the rich man in the story, was able to make an adjustment and live on. But he was not happy there.

## The eternal nature of hell

Jesus said in Matthew 25:46, 'And they will go away into eternal punishment, but the righteous into eternal life.' Hell is not temporary, as the notion of purgatory suggests. The truth is that hell is eternal. Purgatory, the idea of an intermediate testing ground that one can get out of, is not a biblical doctrine. There is absolutely no foundation for it and anyone counting on it will be sadly disappointed.

The dreadfulness of hell is its eternal hopelessness; no torture or punishment need be involved for hell to be what it is. With hope that captivity will end, there is strength to endure, but this will not be so with hell. Without hope, no one can be happy.

## Popular alternatives to hell

Three philosophical doctrines that often function as alternatives to hell in the popular mind are the idea of an immortal soul, karma and reincarnation. They are really more horrifying than hell when duly considered, and offer no real comfort.

## An immortal soul

Soul immortality is of Greek origin. Dualistic Greek thought, that is, the philosophy that the body and all matter are evil while the mind, spirit and soul are good, teaches that the body is a prison for the soul, which survives the death of the body and lives on. This doctrine found its way into the church many centuries after the New Testament was completed and it is still embraced by many today. Despite its widespread popularity, it is an unbiblical doctrine. A possible consequence of believing we have an immortal soul is that we may imagine we are godlike and need not fear judgement or hell.

The Bible does speak of the 'soul' and also of spirit, mind, body, flesh, heart, and so on. But we know we are a whole, and the integration of all the 'parts' into an indivisible whole is biblical. By saying that people have a soul or spirit we are saying that we are spiritual beings, more than mere clay. It also reflects the fact that humans are made in the image of God and are responsible to him.

Soul immortality is a notion readily embraced by adherents of Eastern religions as it dovetails into their beliefs, such as karma and reincarnation.

## Karma and reincarnation

Karma, the cosmic payback programmes, is an extension of the idea of the immortal soul. Within the teaching of karma is the notion that the soul simply continues to exist. There is therefore no hell or heaven, just different forms and modes of existence.

Karma essentially means that 'what goes around, comes around' — to put it in plain language. If I do good, more good than bad, then maybe I will advance in a subsequent life. If I advance enough, I may escape the endless cycle of having to be born repeatedly.

Karma and the attendant doctrine of reincarnation (a continual rebirth) is of human invention; these doctrines, applied in tandem, were a convenient tool used by the ancient Indian upper castes to keep the lower castes in their place. Have you considered the hideous fruit of the doctrines? If you walk the streets of Calcutta, or any other major city in India, you will see it first-hand. Suffering, sick and dying people are left alone in their misery because they are only working out bad karma. Living the good life, like the life of someone in a high caste, is evidence of having overcome bad karma. In addition, death has less significance in such an environment because there will be a reincarnation.

I am amused when people say, 'Reincarnation used to be in the Bible but some church council in the fourth or fifth century took it out.' This is untrue. It is a religious myth akin to the idea that Jesus visited China, India, Tibet or Disneyland, during the so-called 'lost years' (between the ages of twelve and thirty). It may be pointed out that if Jesus had travelled outside of Israel, he rejected whatever he found there since there is no mention or allusion to karma or reincarnation in his teachings.

The teachings of reincarnation, karma and the immortality of the soul are attempts to do away with the awful truth of hell, the proponents of which are surely the blind leading the blind.

## A last word on hell

The Bible teaches that God will give eternal existence to everyone, both the just and the unjust (Acts 24:15). God is the source of all life. Thus, we do not have life in us naturally; we do not have an immortal soul that will survive us at death — we are soul. We have eternal life based on resurrection. Jesus was very clear on this point. It is vital that you see it.

> Truly, truly, I say to you, the hour is coming, and now is, when the dead will hear the voice of the Son of God, and those who hear will live. For as the Father has life in himself, so he has granted the Son also to have life in himself, and has given him authority to execute judgement, because he is the Son of man. Do not marvel at this; for the hour is coming when all who are in the tombs will hear his voice and come forth, those who have done good, to the resurrection of life, and those who have done evil, to the resurrection of judgement (John 5:25–29).

This is clear enough — everyone will be resurrected — some to heaven and some to hell. And let me reiterate: no one will be happy in hell. Though you will exist in the darkness of hell, you will not be happy there.

## Fourth: You have been duped if you think God is too busy to notice

There are many interesting images in the book of Revelation and one of the most fascinating is the 'opening of the books'. John records:

> Then I saw a great white throne and him who sat upon it; from his presence earth and sky fled away, and no place was found for them. And I saw the dead, great and small, standing before the throne, and books were opened. Also another book was opened, which is the book of life. And the dead were judged by what was written in the books, by what they had done. And the sea gave up the dead in it, Death and Hades gave up the dead in them, and all were judged by what they had done. Then Death and Hades were

thrown into the lake of fire. This is the second death, the lake of fire; and if any one's name was not found written in the book of life, he was thrown into the lake of fire (Rev. 20:11–15).

I do not know of a more dreadful passage in Scripture. You would be hard pressed to find more frightening words. It is a most severe warning, but one that must be sounded.

## The warnings

Why are there warnings in Scripture? It would be tempting to delete a number of such passages, but they are there for a reason. We find warnings sprinkled throughout the Scriptures and they are there for our good. What if God did not warn us? Could we say in such an event that he is a just and merciful God? We are warned that the 'books' will be opened.

This reference to the 'books' takes us back into a very Jewish setting. Before the days of Jesus, the Jewish people would speak of the 'books', and they still do, especially orthodox Jews during Yom Kippur. According to ancient Jewish tradition, God inscribed the names of the righteous into a book. The books are a metaphor for God's accounting process, his computer hard drive, his grand database — which is completely accurate and up-to-date.

There are at least two other books in addition to the book of life. These books contain the names of those who are not part of the redeemed community, and a record of what they have done. There is one chief work God requires of us: that we believe in the one whom he sent, who is his only Son, Jesus Christ our Lord. Jesus was asked by a group of people, 'What must we do, to be doing the works of God?' Jesus answered them, 'This is the work of God, that you believe in him whom he has sent' (John 6:28–29). The book of life contains the list of all those who have completed that work.

John is using the word 'books' as a metaphor. I have a hard time envisioning literal books. If John were to have had his revelation in our day, perhaps the books would have been computer discs. You can take it literally or figuratively, but the main point is: God knows. God knows who are his and who are not.

## God knows

Omniscience (all-knowing) is one of the fundamental attributes of God. If we humans, flawed as we are, can develop super-computers, imagine what the Creator can do. The 'books' will one day be opened and you have been duped if you think that God has been too busy to notice you. Once the books are opened, there are no second chances. Any desperate, last-minute pleas for leniency will go unheeded. Can you see yourself standing before God, guilty and without excuse or defence of any kind? If this does not strike fear into you, you are as deceived as you can be.

## Fifth: You have been duped if you think your life cannot change in a 'New York minute'

Luke 19 contains the story of a man named Zacchaeus. The account goes like this: Jesus was travelling through Jericho on his way to Jerusalem, during the second-to-last week of his earthly life. Great crowds of pilgrims were arriving in Jerusalem for the Passover and the twelve apostles, along with a larger group of Jesus' followers, were also present. The local people lined the streets of Jericho waiting to see the man who had so stirred up the hopes of the common people. I imagine it was a wild, noisy and dusty scene.

There was a man in that town named Zacchaeus. He was a tax collector; in fact, he was a chief tax collector. To be a tax collector at that time was to be a traitor — someone who had sold out to Rome.

The Romans were very good at collecting taxes. Based on a census, the Romans would determine how much a given district owed. Then they hired local men to collect the taxes for them. The Romans demanded a certain amount based on the population of an area and allowed the tax collector to keep anything he extorted beyond that. Zacchaeus, being a chief tax collector, would have had a number of others working for him as well. He was hated and despised — probably the number one outcast in the entire city of Jericho.

Zacchaeus had obviously heard about Jesus and for some reason wanted to see him. This was very risky for it meant exposing himself publicly. But, his interest in Jesus was so great that he took the chance.

## Up in a tree

Zacchaeus ran ahead of the procession of pilgrims and climbed into a sycamore tree so that he could see Jesus as he made his way through town. When Jesus got to the tree, he stopped, looked up and saw Zacchaeus. Jesus then said — and no doubt many in the crowd heard him — 'Zacchaeus, come down.'

To go off on a tangent for a moment, how did Jesus know Zacchaeus' name? Well, Jesus would have just known, some say. Maybe, but perhaps someone tapped Jesus on the shoulder and said, 'See, up in the tree, that is Zacchaeus and he is the worst guy in the whole town.' Take your pick, but I choose the latter.

## The tree metaphor

Now Zacchaeus was up in a literal tree. What tree are you in? It was probably greed that got Zacchaeus into such a mess. Maybe he hated the people of Jericho and relished extorting money out of them. Maybe he had a drug or alcohol problem and needed the money to keep up his lifestyle. Maybe he did not care any more, about himself or anyone else, and did not mind being mean and hated. Perhaps he had had a bad experience with the Jewish religious leaders, or maybe he had given up on God. Maybe he was simply self-absorbed and could not think of anyone but himself.

The reason is nothing but a detail; everyone has some story or another. But Jesus stopped by the tree and called, 'Zacchaeus, come down quickly, for I must stay at your house today.' Everything changed for that man in a moment.

Zacchaeus did what Jesus said to do. He came down out of the tree. When you hear the voice of Jesus, you will come down out of your tree. Whatever it is that has deceived you, the call of Jesus clears that away.

We are, indeed, lost and dead and blinded by our sin. We do not see it though — we are that lost, dead and blind.

Who has reasoned your way to God? Who has acquired so much knowledge that you have discovered God? Who was so righteous and devoted that you were able to summon and control God? Salvation is always based on election and revelation. Jesus calls our name. He reveals himself to us. He gives us faith and helps us turn from our sin. Just like Zacchaeus, after Jesus calls you out of your tree, he will say to you, 'I must go to your house today.'

## Fellowship with God

The story of Zacchaeus is a picture of conversion, which is brought about by God's Holy Spirit indwelling us. We become a 'temple' that God himself lives in. We actually have direct and personal fellowship with God.

In the story, Jesus went to Zacchaeus' house. Jesus invited himself. He did not ask Zacchaeus if it was okay. And Jesus took his entire entourage with him — it was going to be quite a celebration.

What an honour it was for Zacchaeus to have the renowned teacher at his house! Jesus risked being condemned by the rest of the people in

Jericho by going to a 'big' sinner's house. Jesus saves us one at a time, and each one is special to him. Jesus does not care what our sins are or how others regard us. He very much wants to forgive and wash our sin away. He is not intent on punishing but in reconciling.

## The joyful reception

How do we know Zacchaeus was genuinely converted? The answer is in the text. He received Jesus joyfully! He brought Jesus home with him. Before that, Zacchaeus had repented. He vowed to give back all the money he had extorted, and more besides. He admitted his dishonesty; he had been a big crook. By the time he made restitution, he would have essentially impoverished himself. His repentance was expensive.

## A 'New York minute'

Zacchaeus received Jesus joyfully — in a moment. It takes a whole lifetime to get ourselves as deceived and lost as we are, but it takes just a 'New York minute' for Jesus to dispel the darkness, penetrate the deception, call our names and bring us to himself. It all happens in an instant and we can only look back on it with amazement. We call it amazing grace — that sweet sound that saves duped people like us.

'It is an easy book to read and I would recommend it to a new Christian
seeking a greater understanding of the Christian faith'
—*The Gospel Magazine*

# Why I am a Christian

## by Kent Philpott

*'Given all the barriers and obstacles that stood in my way I am surprised I became
a Christian at all. There were so many hindrances that, thinking of them now,
I am amazed afresh that I was ever converted.'*

From this starting point Kent Philpott deals with the vital and pertinent questions of why
and how we become Christians. Pointing us to the mercy, grace and divine sovereignty
of God through every trial and difficulty on a Christian's road to salvation he answers
such questions as 'Is life just a gamble?' 'Is sin a disease?' 'What is happening to hell?' In
so doing he takes us through the often painful journey of conviction, repentance and
conversion to a saving faith in our Lord Jesus Christ, showing how it was God himself
who removed the obstacles and overcame the problems that kept us from him.

The book is divided into short, concise chapters and is written in a clear and contemporary
style. The author draws from his own personal experience of salvation, highlighting the
common problems of today that face us all and revealing the need for a total dependence
on God in dealing with them throughout the Christian life.

EVANGELICAL PRESS, ISBN 0 85234 501 1

# From death into life
## by William Haslam

'The parson is converted! The parson is converted!' was the cry from the congregation the day Rev. William Haslam was converted. It happened to this Anglican priest while he was preaching in his own church. This was in Cornwall, England, in the 1840s.

The Rev. Haslam tells the story of his conversion, and so much more, in *From death into life* — newly published by Evangelical Press and Earthen Vessel Publishing.

*Kent Philpott says: 'I have not had a book have such an impact on me in two decades; I have never seen so many people of my personal acquaintance so struck by a book in my lifetime. We simply wanted others to read this incredible story.'*

EVANGELICAL PRESS / EARTHEN VESSEL PUBLISHING, ISBN 0 9703296 2 8

# For pastors of small churches
## by Kent Philpott

Most churches are small churches and they are — and always have been — the backbone of Christianity, despite the emergence of the 'mega' church.

Kent Philpott, himself a long-time pastor, provides practical encouragement to pastors of small and large churches alike. Pastors around the world have found it to be a valuable resource. Published by Earthen Vessel Publishing, and in its second printing, the emphasis throughout the book is that the one thing *all* pastors can do, is preach the gospel of Jesus Christ.

Some of the most popular chapters are: On learning to preach, On being a counselor, Coping with failure, Thoughts on retirement, Angry pastors, and Dragons in the church.

EARTHEN VESSEL PUBLISHING, ISBN 0 9703296 0 1

 Earthen Vessel Publishing

 EVANGELICAL PRESS